The Stroop Report

The Stroop Report

The Jewish Quarter
of Warsaw Is No More!

Translated from the German and Annotated by Sybil Milton
Introduction by Andrzej Wirth

Pantheon Books, New York

All rights reserved under International and Pan-American Copyright
Conventions. Published in the United States by Pantheon Books,
a division of Random House, Inc., New York, and simultaneously
in Canada by Random House of Canada Limited, Toronto.
Originally published in West Germany as
Es gibt keinen jüdischen Wohnbezirk in Warschau mehr
by Hermann Luchterhand Verlag, Neuwied, West Germany.

Library of Congress Cataloging in Publication Data

Stroop, Juergen, 1895-
The Stroop report.

Translation of Es gibt keinen jüdischen Wohnbezirk in
Warschau mehr.
1. Warsaw—History—Uprising of 1943—Personal
narratives. 2. Stroop, Juergen, 1895-   I. Title.
D765.2.W3S78613   940.53'438'4   79-1900
ISBN 0-394-50443-7

Manufactured in the United States of America

FIRST AMERICAN EDITION

CONTENTS

Introduction
by Andrzej Wirth

I

This edition of the *Stroop Report* is appearing nineteen years after the publication of the first German facsimile edition (Luchterhand, 1960) and three years after the German paperback edition (Sammlung Luchterhand, 1976). I was editorially responsible for the German editions. Publication of the *Report* in 1960 required some courage and persistence. Many, at that time, considered the uncomfortable past mastered at least in theory and did not want to hear any more about it. The German edition finally appeared thanks to the efforts of the writer Guenter Grass as well as those of the undersigned. I was then cultural editor of the Warsaw weekly *Polityka*, and Poland was the official depository of the *Report*.

Several photographs from the *Stroop Report* have in the meantime been widely publicized by the international media, and they now constitute a readily available pictorial archive of the history of mass crime. The Pantheon facsimile edition reproduces these photographs in their original context, which shows the incredible meanings that they were assigned under the Nazi system of thought.

The *Stroop Report* looks like a family album, a dignified commemorative volume bound in black pebble leather. The title page, in Gothic calligraphy, reads "The Jewish quarter of Warsaw is no more!"

The *Report* consists of three parts: a descriptive narrative introduction; daily communiqués on the progress of the "operation"; and a series of photographs. The first part of the *Report* was typed on white, glossy, deckle-edged Bristol paper. The pages are not numbered and have writing on one side only. This part ends with Stroop's signature.

The second part of the *Report* consists of the copies that were made of the thirty-two detailed communiqués, which Stroop transmitted by daily telegraph to Krueger, Higher SS and Police Leader East in Cracow. These communiqués span the period from 20 April to 16 May 1943. They were typed on both sides of plain paper.

SS-Sturmbannfuehrer (Major) Jesuiter, Chief of Staff of the SS and Police Leader in the Warsaw District (i.e., Stroop's Chief of Staff) certified that the copies of all daily communiqués matched the originals. His signature is affixed to the lower left-hand corner of the last page of each communiqué.

The third part of the *Report* consists of fifty-four photographs on white Bristol paper; thirty-nine of the photos are captioned in Gothic script.

In 1948, Stroop himself explained to the Central Commission for the Investigation of War Crimes in Poland how the *Report* came into existence. Further testimony was provided to the American occupation authorities in Wiesbaden in 1946 by Stroop's adjutant, Karl Kaleske. The testimony shows that the daily communiqués on the progress of the Ghetto operation were teletyped to Cracow on Krueger's instructions; they were then forwarded to SS-Chief Himmler, who had ordered both the Warsaw operation and Stroop's transfer from Lemberg to direct it. After the liquidation of the Ghetto, Krueger

expressed the wish that a complete set of the communiqués be sent to Himmler as a memento. This is how the album that we know as the *Stroop Report* was created.

Three sets of this document were assembled. The first was presented to Himmler; Krueger received the second; and Stroop kept the third. According to Stroop, the set that has been deposited with the Central Commission for the Investigation of War Crimes in Poland is the one that Himmler had received. It was found at the end of the war by soldiers of the U.S. 7th Army.

Stroop never contested the authenticity of the document shown to him in the course of his trial proceedings. The *Stroop Report* was submitted in evidence in 1946 before the International Military Tribunal in Nuremberg, in 1947 before the American Military Tribunal in Nuremberg, and finally in 1951 before the District Court of the Capital City of Warsaw in the trial of Juergen Stroop and others.

II

The Stroop album is the classical product of an obsession with documentation in our technological age. Everything is inventoried and documented by the bureaucratic machine—and mass murder is no exception. The daily communiqués sent by teletype to Krueger in Cracow are pedantic, factual, professional, and expressed in figures. Mass murder is abstracted into a statistical *quantity*: "The total number of Jews apprehended has risen to 55,885" [*Die Gesamtzahl der erfassten Juden erhoeht sich auf 55.885*]. The count includes attack and blockade forces, losses, booty, ammunition, and "bunkers" [*Bunker*] blown up.

However, the reader should critically examine some of Stroop's statistics. Stroop tried to minimize his own losses, perhaps to impress his superiors. The casualty list probably included only the names of those who were to be decorated posthumously. The Polish underground estimated that between 400 and 700 Germans were killed or wounded. The report is also silent about the fact that during the Ghetto revolt and after that, until October 1944, Poles arrested in the "Aryan" part of the city were routinely taken to the Ghetto for liquidation. According to information provided by Kazimierz Moczarski, the number of Jews who were murdered during the Ghetto revolt and the number of Poles who were then or subsequently killed was the same—about 20,000 each. In fact, the largest mass execution of Poles, approximately 575 men and women, took place in the Ghetto on 30 May 1943.

In the end, the report became the victim of its own obsession with numbers. The booty of more than a month's "battle" between almost 2,000 troops and 60,000 "Jews and bandits" [*Juden und Banditen*] is startlingly sparse: "7 Polish rifles, 1 USSR rifle, 1 German rifle, 59 pistols of various calibers, several hundred hand grenades, including Polish and handmade ones, a few hundred incendiary bottles, homemade explosives, and time bombs with fuses."

The author of the *Report* felt compelled to explain "that in most cases arms could not be taken." The idea of total utilization [*Verwertung*] also becomes evident here: "The hand grenades, explosives, and incendiary bottles captured by us were immediately put to use against the bandits."

Complete documentation in the contemporary style would probably have included tape recordings of the screams of the dying; the live telecast of the

"liquidation" of the Symbionese Liberation Army and much of the coverage of the Vietnam War with its daily body count approached this ideal. The *Stroop Report* still had to rely on old-fashioned methods of documentation, which were limited to interpretative or descriptive words and photo-stills. Most of the pictures prove to be "gestural" in the Brechtian sense of the word, *gestus* conveying a basic behavioral attitude. While this was apparently an unintentional effect, most of the photographs have a clear gestural impact, which frequently contradicts the meta-linguistic smoke screen of the captions. Thus the caption "Pulled from the bunkers by force" is contradicted by a photo showing women, children, and the aged surrounded by armed men in helmets; the statement that the Jews "led a splendid existence" in their "residential bunkers" is contradicted by photos of miserable hovels; the dignity and beauty of the "bandits' faces" points up the ugliness of their persecutors; the sea of flames and arson stands out as the chief weapon of the pacifiers; "the battle" reveals itself as a manhunt: note the grotesqueness of a combat patrol, strutting through the burning streets, guns pointed at women and children.

In the terminology of semiotics, the pictures are object-language and the captions their semantic paraphrase or meta-language. The real message of the *Stroop Report* lies in the tension and conflict of the two languages.

III

The language of fascism appears in the *Stroop Report* practically unfiltered through any kind of ideological screen; it is precise and direct for its purposes, even though it represents a distortion of German usage. It is the lingua of the technological age, to be studied for its use in relation to mass murder.

It is interesting that even in Stroop's more ideological introduction the term "final solution" [*Endlösung*] remains taboo; he writes about mass resettlements whose purpose or result is not mentioned. Mass resettlements were *idées fixes* of both Hitler and Stalin. In the lingua of the *Stroop Report*, they are called "transfers" [*Verlagerung*], an ingenious word for what it describes—the road from a transit camp to an extermination camp, with the latter usually referred to only by code number, e.g., T II for Treblinka.

The following synonyms were used to describe the place of forced Jewish residential segregation: "the Jewish quarter" [*der juedische Wohnbezirk*], "ghetto" or " remnant ghetto" [*Restghetto*], "quarantine district" [*Seuchensperrgebiet*], "reservation" [*Sammelbecken*], "confinement" [*Zusammenballung*]. "Transported onward" [*abtransportiert*] and "transferred" [*verlagert*] are both euphemisms for a course of action whose aim, disguised in meta-language, was to "protect the Aryan population from the Jews" [*die arische Bevoelkerung vor den Juden zu schuetzen*].

Just as perverse is the use of the adjective "voluntary." Behavior which bends to the will of the master race is "voluntary." This makes the following sentence possible: "The Jews no longer considered *voluntary* resettlement but were determined to resist with all weapons and means at their disposal" [*Die Juden keinesfalls an eine freiwillige Umsiedlung dachten, sondern gewillt waren, sich mit allen Moeglichkeiten und den ihnen zur Verfuegung stehenden Waffen zur Wehr zu setzen*]. (Emphasis added.)

The destruction of the Warsaw Ghetto reached its symbolic end when the synagogue was blown up. Also symbolic was the fact that Dzielna-Prison of the Security Police was spared in order "to change [it] into a concentration

camp and to use the prisoners to strip down and collect the millions of bricks, scrap iron, and other materials for further utilization."

The recurring use of the word "utilization" [*Verwertung*] is important, for it exemplifies the dialectic reasoning of fascism: the negativeness of destruction must give way to the positive—the "utilization" of remaining parts that are integrated into a new synthesis, even if that involves the conversion of a prison into a concentration camp.

The opponents of the Ghetto operation are described in combinations of incompatible terms—"Jews and bandits" or "Jews and criminals"—and their identification becomes uncertain; for example: "180 Jews, bandits, and sub-humans were destroyed" [*Es wurden 180 Juden, Banditen und Untermenschen vernichtet*]. Ghetto residents are referred to as "bunker occupants" [*Insassen*], "gangs" [*Banden*], "bandits" [*Banditen*], "lowest elements" [*niedrigste Elemente*], "rabble and subhumanity" [*Gesindel und Untermenschen*], and "creatures" [*Kreaturen*]. But when the time comes for giving final statistics, the report simply speaks of Jews: "6,929 Jews were destroyed via transport to T II" [*Durch Transport nach T.II wurden 6.929 Juden vernichtet*]. "Destroyed via transport"—the language of bureaucratic mass murder reaches its peak in this striving for economy of expression.

The report speaks of "bunkers" in the Ghetto, and the implication of a military engagement is retained almost consistently. The impression is created of combat against military bunkers. But then the report speaks of "residential bunkers" [*Wohnbunker*] (teletype message of 29 April). The lost military implication is thereupon restored by a reference to "bunker crews" (previously called bunker occupants): "Statements made by various bunker crews revealed that these Jews have not been outside for the last 10 days and that they are running short on food, etc., due to the extended duration of the grand operation" [*Aus den Aussagen verschiedener Bunkerbesatzungen geht hervor dass die Juden bereits 10 Tage nicht mehr aus denselben hervorgekommen sind, und dass ihnen nun infolge der laengeren Dauer der Grossaktion die Lebensmittel usw. ausgehen*].

The attempt to describe the "Ghetto operation," or "grand operation" as it was later called, as a military engagement constantly involves the author of the report in new difficulties. Thus the *Report* speaks of "sweeping" [*Durchkaemmung*], "operation" [*Einsatz*], "search" [*Durchsuchung*], "tracking down" [*Aufspuerung*], "blowing-up" [*sprengen*], "crushing" [*niederkaempfen*], "destroying" [*vernichten*], "penetrating" [*eindringen*], and "routing-out" [*aufstoebern*]. It invents imaginative phraseology like "disposed of in battle" [*kampfmaessig erledigt*] and "dropped out due to wounds" [*Ausfall durch Verwundung*]. (Jews in the *Report*, incidentally, are either *dead* or alive, but rarely wounded.)

Yet, the *Report* cannot avoid the use of a second object-language, the object-language of mass murder. We then read of "attack or [*beziehungsweise*] blow-up" [*zu bekaempfen bzw. zu sprengen*]; "Jews apprehended or [*beziehungsweise*] destroyed" [*erfassten bzw. vernichteten Juden*]. The German adverb *beziehungsweise* is significant because it makes possible the transformation of an item of information into a contradictory item of information. Linguistically, it makes the coexistence of two "object-terminologies" possible: a military terminology and a terminology of mass murder, whereby the former functions as a meta-linguistic paraphrase of the latter.

Finally, the object-language of bureaucracy becomes an auxiliary tool

whenever the other two terminologies prove inadequate. "In this connection, it will be of interest that an illegal ammunition cache exploded in a burning building in the very district in which we are *doing work*" [*Hierbei interessiert die Tatsache, dass bei einem Brand eines Gebaeudes, in dem z.Zt.* bearbeiteten *Wohnbezirk, ein illegales Munitionslager in die Luft ging*]. (Emphasis added.) Mass murder was assimilated into the work ethic of fascism; the nations on its death list are objects for diligent work [*Bearbeitung*] and utilization [*Verwertung*]. Stroop receives a hero's medal, the Iron Cross First Class, "in recognition for services rendered in his *work* in Warsaw." (Emphasis added.)

The absurd logic of totalitarian wishful thinking ("only what should exist does exist") is noticeable in the use of the term "so-called" [*sogenannt*]. "The *so-called* library, located outside the Ghetto, was placed at their disposal for temporary storage of raw materials, etc." [*Zur vorlaeufigen Lagerung der Rohstoffe usw. wurde die* sog. *Bibliothek ausserhalb des Ghettos zur Verfuegung gestellt*]. (Emphasis added.) The library is acceptable only as something else and is arbitrarily designated as a raw materials depot. The same formula is applied to people and to objects: "I decide who is a Jew; I also decide what is a raw materials depot." The fascist usurps for himself an absolute right to the idiosyncratic use of language.

IV

The *Stroop Report* deals with one particular phase of the "final solution," the Nazis' name for their genocidal program for European Jews. This phase was *unique*, an isolated instance of organized Jewish resistance against extermination, after the population of the Warsaw Ghetto had been reduced by daily deportations from almost half a million to about 60,000 survivors. The historian and eye-witness Emanuel Ringelblum wrote that "the 'resettlement' should not have been permitted. We should have run out into the streets, set fire to everything in sight, torn down the walls, escaped to the Other Side. The Germans would have taken their revenge. It would have cost tens of thousands of lives, but not 300,000. Now we are ashamed of ourselves, disgraced in our own eyes and in the eyes of the world, where our docility earned us nothing. This must not be repeated now. We must put up a resistance, defend ourselves against the enemy, man and child." [Quoted from L. Tushnet, *To Die with Honor* (New York, 1965)].

Sealed ghettos and extermination camps were the means for organized genocide. Warsaw was the largest ghetto and served as a concentration and transit camp for the Jews who were being deported from the cities of central Poland. Modes of extermination in a Ghetto included overcrowding (the population of the Warsaw Ghetto grew from 160,000 to half a million), epidemics, and starvation. In the summer of 1941, the monthly death rate was 5,500. The mode of extermination in the camps was the gas chamber. In the summer of 1942, the SS announced the "Resettlement to the East" [*Verlagerung nach Osten*]. What was meant was the extermination camp in Treblinka. For nine weeks, 5-6,000 people per day (including hospital patients and orphans) were deported in freight trains (100 persons in each boxcar). In Treblinka, they marched to the gas chambers, where 200 people were gassed at a time.

The immediate cause of the Ghetto revolt in April 1943 was Himmler's order (of 16 February 1943) finally to liquidate the remainder of the Jewish

Quarter. At this stage, the survivors in the Ghetto had no doubts as to the real purpose of the "Resettlement to the East." Traveling a circuitous route, news of the fate of the masses of earlier deportees had reached the isolated Ghetto.

The ZOB (Zydowska Organizacja Bojowa/Jewish Fighting Organization) and the affiliated ZZW (Zydowski Zwiazek Wojskowy/Jewish Military Union) formed the core of resistance, both commanded by the 24-year-old Mordechai Anielewicz. Toward the end of February, the ZOB was counting twenty-two fighting groups, each consisting of twenty to thirty men and women between the ages of 18 and 25. Their weapons consisted of revolvers, ten to fifteen pieces of ammunition, four or five hand grenades, and Molotov cocktails. Each group had two or three rifles, and there was *one* machine gun for the entire fighting organization.

Jewish armed resistance would be impossible without outside help. On April 30, the plenipotentiary of the Polish exile government issued an appeal to the Polish nation to give the persecuted Jews all help possible under the circumstances. On May 5, the prime minister, General Sikorski, in a speech broadcast from London, stated that "the gravest crime in the history of mankind is taking place. We know that you try to provide relief to the Jewish martyrs. I beg you to give them all possible assistance and at the same time to eradicate this frightful atrocity." (W. Bartoszewski, *1859 Dsni Warszawy* [*1859 Days in Warsaw*], Cracow, 1974). The AK (Armja Krajowa/Home Army), the chief Polish resistance organization directed by the exiled Polish government, provided relief on several occasions and participated in the smuggling of weapons and explosives into the Ghetto. Organized assistance was also rendered by the GL (Gwardia Ludowa/People's Guard), which had links to the PPR, the pro-Soviet Communist party. Immanent in the text of the *Stroop Report* is further evidence of help provided by Poles to the Jewish fighters in the repeated references to "Jews and Polish bandits."

SS-Oberfuehrer (Brigadier General) von Sammern-Frankenegg was entrusted with the task of final liquidation of the Ghetto, which meant the deportations and assuring the safety of machines and products of several private German factories that were using Ghetto Jews as slave laborers. 19 April was the date designated for the final "operation"; this was the first day of Passover of the Jewish calendar. It was obvious that Himmler had chosen the liquidation of the Ghetto as Adolf Hitler's birthday present. The frontal attack by the troops commanded by von Sammern-Frankenegg, however, was repulsed by the surprise Jewish counterattack. The attackers suffered losses and withdrew in panic. The following day, command was transferred to SS-Brigadefuehrer (Major-General) Juergen Stroop, who had recently arrived from Galicia.

V

Who was Juergen Stroop? His SS biography is derived from his personnel dossier that the Americans deposited in the Berlin Document Center. His career made a brilliant and meteoric ascent, catapulting Stroop from a civil service, lower-middle-class milieu into the exclusive club of the SS elite. Stroop returned from the First World War as a Vizefeldwebel (Vice-Sergeant). In 1934, his rank in the SS was sergeant. Five years later, he had advanced to the rank of SS Oberfuehrer (Brigadier-General) and Oberst der Schutzpolizei (Colonel in the Police). His education ended with secondary school. He was

the son of a policeman and became an expert in the pacification of the civilian population of the occupied lands of Czechoslovakia, Soviet Russia, Poland, and Greece. Notwithstanding this background, Stroop was fond of picturing himself as a professional front-line officer with a nostalgic weakness for horseback riding, monocle, and uniform, but at heart he was a policeman, not a military man.

The main source for an understanding of Stroop's personality is a posthumously published book by Kazimierz Moczarski, *Conversations with the Hangman (Gespraeche mit dem Henker)*, Warsaw 1977. The author, one of the heroes of the Polish resistance and an officer of the AK, was thrown into jail without a trial for eleven years by the Polish Stalinists; in 1949 he was locked into the same cell with Stroop. (The cynical preface to the Polish edition of the book reads "*Fate* threw Stroop into the same jail cell with Kazimierz Moczarski.") (Emphasis added.)

Moczarski thought that cruelty was integral to Stroop's personality but that Stroop was unaware of his cruelty. In conversation Stroop appeared limited, low in intelligence, poorly educated; his ideological motivations are revealed in Nazi slogans. He was an authoritarian personality, combining the desire for dominance over others with the need for subordination to a powerful authority.

Stroop, who was raised a Catholic by his mother, changed his first name from Josef to Juergen in 1941 and listed his religious affiliation as "believer." His maxims were: orders are orders; my virtue is loyalty; order must prevail. His religiosity was conventional, his love of family was emphatic. Worship of authority and power was linked in Stroop with servility and submissiveness. Stroop said to Moczarski in their prison cell: "Mr. Moczarski, you are the representative of a victorious people who are the government here, therefore a superior race [*Herrenvolk*]." This volunteer of the First World War remained a worshipper of uniforms and war, a combat mentality through and through. His military ideal was General Erich Ludendorff; his anti-Semitic ideas came from Dr. Mathilde Ludendorff. He confused liberalism with anarchy and was a sworn enemy of the Weimar Republic, which was too anarchistic for him. For Stroop the core of national being was ideological, the dictatorship of the Fuehrer and blind obedience, the latter functioning as a kind of therapy.

Stroop's espousal of the principle of obedience was not able to exculpate him before an American court in Dachau and a Polish tribunal in Warsaw. Both courts adhered to their own principle, not to punish merely the most immediate perpetrators of a crime ("chain of command principle"). Stroop's first death sentence for the shooting of American pilots was signed by General L.D. Clay; the Polish court judged his activity in Poland a "continuous crime" and branded him a "fascist hangman."

In conversations with Moczarski conducted in the gallows' shadow (both prisoners were expecting the death sentence), Stroop confessed what the courts did not know: that he had also had a hand in the stage suicide of Field Marshal General von Kluge.

Moczarski's notes portray Stroop as a Nazi functionary who combined a puritanical devotion to discipline with an idealistic sense of mission, a man unable to differentiate between legality and morality. These notes also reveal a highly self-disciplined person with a perverted group loyalty that excluded

any trace of human solidarity. Greatness was lacking in this executor of great crime. This is what makes him frightening. No evil demon, he was perhaps only a functionary of evil, masquerading as law. Stroop's most striking characteristic may have been his coldness, what Moczarski called the "lead in Stroop's eyes."

VI

Who were Juergen Stroop's opponents? Desperadoes, heroes, lunatics? Beginning in July 1942, the Warsaw Ghetto became a waiting room for slaughter. The physician Marek Edelman, one of the leaders of the revolt and the only surviving member of its leadership, talks of the meaning to be found in a hopeless struggle (H. Krall, *Zdażyć przed Panem Bogiem* [*Making It Before God*], Warsaw, 1977). He argues that the individual right to death is a traditional canon of human culture, and he regards the belief that death is more beautiful with a weapon in one's hand than without as an elementary human convention. It is significant that he does not speak of "heroism" but of "fireworks," meaning that for its participants the Ghetto revolt was a symbolic act of solidarity with the world *beyond* the wall. Edelman's point is that because the Nazis had denied the incarcerated their humanity, it had to be proven anew. However, I assume that this is not to be understood as a categorical imperative. The activists who resisted merely responded in a different way to the same force of compulsion than those who passively walked to the *Umschlagplatz*. Passive death is no less worthy than an activist death. Our moral intuition prevents us from passing judgment. Walls, racism, and creating divisions between their victims were the tools the Nazis employed to rob the incarcerated of their fundamental freedom, their equality with humanity, and their ethnological brotherhood. Under such conditions of compulsion, without precedence in European cultural memory, the death of a rebel became an act of solidarity with the outside world (where choice over the manner of death was considered a basic freedom), and death in the gas chambers was an act of solidarity as well with the incarcerated.

VII

In 1943, the Warsaw Ghetto became the drill ground for the "final solution." Nazi propaganda intimated that the Germans would solve the "Jewish question" for the Poles and for all time. Nearly 400 Polish Order Police are listed among the auxiliary troops in the Ghetto operation. One must remember, however, that the so-called dark-blue police were considered collaborators by the Poles and that many were shot by the Polish underground as traitors.

One year later, in August, the "final solution" was imposed by the Nazis on Warsaw itself. With the Red Army positioned on the right bank of the Vistula in the role of passive observer, Warsaw was sealed off, "walled up," and transformed into a ghetto. Admittedly there was an armed uprising, and a desperate street battle was waged by the underground (AK and AL), which lasted for two long months. However, the methods of destruction the Nazis used were the same. In October 1944 the entire population was forcibly expelled, "transported onward" [*abtransportiert*], and "transferred" [*verlagert*]. With every fourth inhabitant of Warsaw buried under the rubble, the motto

of the *Stroop Report* could have been rewritten "Warsaw is no more!"

The mass executions, the use of heavy arms against a civilian population, the setting of fires, the gassing and dynamiting of sewers where people had sought refuge—these methods of the Ghetto "grand operation" were perfected and used on a larger scale, this time against "Poles and bandits."

Barely twenty years later a key idea of the *Stroop Report, Die Vermauerung* (the walling-up) celebrated its resurrection, this time in the life of the two postwar German states. With the construction of the Berlin Wall, meta-language and object-language were fused, and history recorded a new tragedy, though one not lacking in irony.

Andrzej Wirth

The Stroop Report

Es gibt keinen
jüdischen Wohnbezirk
~ in Warschau mehr !

THE JEWISH QUARTER OF WARSAW IS NO MORE!

Für den Führer und
für ihr Vaterland

sind im Kampf bei der Vernichtung von Juden und Banditen
im ehemaligen jüdischen Wohnbezirk in Warschau gefallen:

Am 20.4.43 SS-Pz.Gren. Paul Jäger, geb. 14.1.25, 4.SS-Pz.Gren.Ers.Abt.
          Gefr. Joseph Strupp, geb. 16.3.07, L.A.Batr. III/8 Flak
          Schütze Christian Hohbein, geb. 23.7.00, L.A.Batr. III/8 Flak

am 22.4.43 SS-Ustuf. Otto Dehmke, geb. 4.7.21, SS-Kav.-Ers.-Abt.
          Wachmann Willi Stark, geb. 4.4.20, Ausb.L.Trawniki
          Wachmann Borys Odartschenko, geb.11.1.23, Ausb.L.Trawniki

am 1.5.43 Rttwm.d.Schp. Hans-J. Bolze, geb. 9.10.20, III/SS-Pol. 22
          SS-Rttf. Edmund Lotholz, geb. 1.11.04, Sicherheitspolizei

am 6.5.43 Obw.d.Schp. Horst Riemer, geb. 10.5.08, I/SS-Pol. 22
          Wm. d.Schp. Rudolf Hartmann, geb. 8.6.09, I/SS-Pol. 22

am 8.5.43 SS-Pz.Gren. Lorenz Bichler, geb. 21.10.24, 2.SS-Pz.Gren.E.B.
          SS-Pz.Gren. Helmut Hinz, geb. 27.4.25, 4. SS-Pz.Gren.Ers.Btl.

am 11.5.43 SS-Strm. Heinz Lehmann, geb. 16.2.12, 1. SS-Pz.Gren.Ers.Btl.

am 13.5.43 SS-Pz.Gren. Heinz Stüwe, geb. 30.11.24, 3. SS-Pz.Gren.Ers.Btl.
          SS-Pz.Gren. Gernard Fritz, geb. 25.4.24, 3. SS-Pz.Gren.Ers.Btl.

Ferner fiel in Ausübung seines Dienstes am 19.4.43 der
          poln. Pol.-Hptw.Julian Zielinski, geb.13.11.91, 14. Komm.

Sie setzten Ihr Höchstes, ihr Leben, ein. Wir werden sie nie vergessen.

For Fuehrer and Fatherland [1]

The following fell in the battle to destroy the Jews and bandits in the former Jewish quarter of Warsaw:

On 20 April 1943
>   SS Panzer Grenadier Paul Jaeger, born 14 January 1925, SS Panzer Grenadier Reserve Division
>   Corporal Joseph Strupp, born 16 March 1907, Light Artillery Anti-aircraft Alarm Battery No. III/8
>   Private Christian Hohbein, born 23 July 1900, Light Artillery Anti-aircraft Alarm Battery No. III/8

On 22 April 1943
>   SS Second Lieutenant Otto Dehmke, born 4 July 1921, SS Cavalry Reserve Division
>   Guard Willi Stark, born 4 April 1920, Trawniki Training Camp
>   Guard Borys Odartschenko, born 11 January 1923, Trawniki Training Camp

On 1 May 1943
>   Corporal of the Protective Police Hans J. Bolze, born 9 October 1920, SS Police Regiment No. 22, 3d Battalion
>   SS Corporal Edmund Lotholz, born 1 November 1904, Security Police

On 6 May 1943
>   Staff Sergeant of the Protective Police Horst Riemer, born 10 May 1908, SS Police Regiment No. 22, 1st Battalion
>   Sergeant of the Protective Police Rudolf Hartmann, born 8 June 1909, SS Police Regiment No. 22, 1st Battalion

On 8 May 1943
>   SS Panzer Grenadier Lorenz Bichler, born 21 October 1924, 2nd SS Panzer Grenadier Reserve Battalion
>   SS Panzer Grenadier Helmut Hinz, born 25 April 1925, 4th SS Panzer Grenadier Reserve Battalion No. 4

On 11 May 1943
>   SS Private First Class Heinz Lehmann, born 16 February 1912, 1st SS Panzer Grenadier Reserve Battalion

On 13 May 1943
>   SS Panzer Grenadier Heinz Stuwe, born 30 November 1924, 3d SS Panzer Grenadier Reserve Battalion
>   SS Panzer Grenadier Gerhard Fritz, born 25 April 1924, 3d SS Panzer Grenadier Reserve Battalion

In addition, the Polish Police Sergeant-Major Julian Zielinski, born 13 November 1891, 14th Commissariat, was killed on 19 April 1943 while carrying out his duties.

They gave their utmost, their lives. We shall never forget them.

Es wurden verwundet

am 19.4.43 SS-Pz.Gren. Wilhelm Schneider, geb.25.1.25, 2.SS-Pz.Gren.Ers.Btl.
SS-Pz.Gren. Friedrich Scholz, geb. 2.6.10, 1.SS-Pz.Gren.Ers.Btl
SS-Pz.Gren. Karl Gnant, geb. 31.7.07, 2. SS-Pz.Gren.Ers.Btl.
SS-Reiter Oskar Reinke, geb.26.8.24, SS-Kav.-Ers.-Abt.
SS-Reiter Alex Wissinger, geb. 11.11.24, SS-Kav.-Ers.-Abt.
SS-Reiter Johannes Neugebauer, geb. 6.3.12, SS-Kav.-Ers.-Abt.
SS-Reiter Anton Imgrund, geb. 22.9.22, SS-Kav.-Ers.-Abt.
SS-Reiter Günther Reitzig, geb.7.11.24, SS-Kav.-Ers.-Abt.
SS-Reiter Franz Strobl, geb. 2.3.22, SS-Kav.-Ers.-Abt.
SS-Strm. Heinz Kruse, geb. 4.12.22, SS-Kav.-Ers.-Abt.
SS-Reiter Anton Müller, geb. 2.12.21, SS-Kav.-Ers.-Abt.
SS-Strm. Johann Tyreck, geb. 6.2.20, SS-Kav.-Ers.-Abt.
SS-Reiter Friedrich Böhm, geb. 8.11.16, SS-Kav.-Ers.-Abt.
SS-Reiter Karl Zechmeister, geb. 5.3.15, SS-Kav.-Ers.-Abt.

SS-Sturmscharf. Rudolf Kosmala, geb.31.10.01, Sicherheitspol.
SS-Rttf. Fritz Rührenschopf, geb. 21.8.10, Sicherheitspolizei

Wachmann Paul Nestarenko, geb.17.8.19, Ausb.L.Tr.Trawniki
Wachmann Andrej Dawidenko, geb.31.1.23, Ausb.L.Tr.Trawniki
Wachmann Michael Minenko, geb. 11.2.21, Ausb.L.Tr.Trawniki
Wachmann Nikolai Huzulak, geb. 16.3.23, Ausb.L.Tr.Trawniki
Wachmann Borys Roschdestwenskyj,geb.10.4.14,Ausb.L.Tr.Trawniki
Wachmann Andrej Prottschenko, geb.1.10.22,Ausbl.L.Tr.Trawniki

poln. Pol.Wm. Franziszek Kluzniski, geb. 30.1.13,7.Komm.
poln. Pol.Mstr. Waclaw Frydrykewicz,geb. 16.5.04,1.Komm.

am 20.4.43 SS-Pz.Gren. Alfons Hausa, geb.10.5.12, 2.SS-Pz.Gren.Ers.Btl.
SS-Pz.Gren. Valentin Malle, geb. 13.2.13, 2.SS-Pz.Gren.Ers.Btl.
SS-Reiter Ludwig Schay, geb. 30.11.22, SS-Kav.-Ers.-Abt.
SS-Reiter Anton Heist, geb. 7.9.21, SS-Kav.-Ers.-Abt.

Wm.d.Schp. Wilhelm Clemm, geb.3.2.43, III./SS-Pol. 22
Obw.d.Schp. Kurt Sprotte, geb.11.9.07, I./SS-Pol. 22
Wm.d.Schp. Rudolf Kreuz, geb. 25.10.08, I./SS-Pol. 22

Feldwebel Joseph Siegert, geb.12.2.97, Eisenb.Pz.E.Abt.
Pi.Kdo.Rembertow

The following were wounded:

On 19 April 1943

SS Panzer Grenadier Wilhelm Schneider, born 25 January 1925, 2nd SS Panzer Grenadier Reserve Battalion

SS Panzer Grenadier Friedrich Scholz, born 2 June 1910, 1st SS Panzer Grenadier Reserve Battalion

SS Panzer Grenadier Karl Gnant, born 31 July 1907, 2nd SS Panzer Grenadier Reserve Battalion

SS Trooper Oskar Reinke, born 26 August 1924, SS Cavalry Reserve Division

SS Trooper Alex Wissinger, born 11 November 1924, SS Cavalry Reserve Division

SS Trooper Johannes Neugebauer, born 6 March 1912, SS Cavalry Reserve Division

SS Trooper Anton Imgrund, born 22 September 1922, SS Cavalry Reserve Division

SS Trooper Guenther Reitzig, born 7 November 1924, SS Cavalry Reserve Division

SS Trooper Franz Strobl, born 2 March 1922, SS Cavalry Reserve Division

SS Private First Class Heinz Kruse, born 4 December 1922, SS Calvary Reserve Division

SS Trooper Anton Mueller, born 2 December 1921, SS Cavalry Reserve Division

SS Private First Class Johann Tyreck, born 6 February 1920, SS Cavalry Reserve Division

SS Trooper Friedrich Boehm, born 8 November 1916, SS Cavalry Reserve Division

SS Trooper Karl Zechmeister, born 5 March 1915, SS Cavalry Reserve Division

SS Sergeant-Major Rudolf Kosmala, born 31 October 1901, Security Police

SS Corporal Fritz Ruehrenschopf, born 21 August 1910, Security Police

Guard Paul Nestarenko, born 17 August 1919, Trawniki Training Camp

Guard Andrej Dawidenko, born 31 January 1923, Trawniki Training Camp

Guard Michael Minenko, born 11 February 1921, Trawniki Training Camp

Guard Nikolai Huzulak, born 16 March 1923, Trawniki Training Camp

Guard Borys Roschdestwenskyj, born 10 April 1914, Trawniki Training Camp

Guard Andrej Prottschenko, born 1 October 1922, Trawniki Training Camp

Polish Police Sergeant Franziszek Kluzniski, born 30 January 1913, 7th Commissariat

Polish Police Sergeant-Major Waclaw Frydrykewicz, born 16 May 1904, 1st Commissariat

On 20 April 1943

SS Panzer Grenadier Alfons Hausa, born 10 May 1912, 2nd SS Panzer Grenadier Reserve Battalion

SS Panzer Grenadier Valentin Malle, born 13 February 1913, 2nd SS Panzer Grenadier Reserve Battalion

SS Trooper Ludwig Schay, born 30 November 1922, SS Cavalry Reserve Division

SS Trooper Anton Heist, born 7 September 1921, SS Cavalry Reserve Division

Sergeant of the Protective Police Wilhelm Clemm, born 3 February 1943 [sic], SS Police Regiment 22, 3d Battalion

Staff Sergeant of the Protective Police Kurt Sprotte, born 11 September 1907, SS Police Regiment No. 22, 1st Battalion

Sergeant of the Protective Police Rudolf Kreuz, born 25 October 1908, SS Police Regiment No. 22, 1st Battalion

Technical Sergeant Joseph Siegert, born 12 February 1897, Engineers Detail of the Railway Armored Trains—Reserve Division Rembertow

SS-Oscha. Sepp Mayowski, geb.23.12.14, Ausb.L.Trawniki

poln.Pol.Wm. Boleslaw Gruschecki, geb. 1.6.14,Gel.u.Wach-Abt.

am 21.4.43 SS-Reiter Johann Lebisch, geb.6.6.21, SS-Kav.-Ers.-Abt.
Zugwm.d.Schp. Kurt Szesnik, geb. 9.11.09, III/SS-Pol. 22
Zugwm.d.Schp. Erich Pärschke, geb. 30.12.14, I/SS-Pol. 22

Wachmann Iwan Knyhynyzkyj, geb. 21.7.23, Ausb.L. Trawniki

am 22.4.43 Zugwm.d.Schp. Otto Koglin, geb. 3.4.11, I/SS-Pol. 22

am 23.4.43 Zugwm.d.Schp. Erich Waclawik, geb. 25.4.10, III/SS-Pol. 22
Wm.d.Schp.d.R. Karl Neidhard, geb. 14.3.03, III/SS-Pol. 22

Wachmann Emil Schmidt, geb. 2.2.23, Ausb.L. Trawniki

am 24.4.43 SS-Uscha. Franz Lüdke, geb. 22.10.22, 1.SS-Pz.Gren.Ers.Btl.
SS-Pz.Gren. Siegfried Böckmann, geb.14.10.12, 1.SS-Pz.Gren.E.B.

Gruppen-Wm. Wladimir Usik, geb. 16.6.17, Ausb.L.Trawniki

am 25.4.43 SS-Pz.Gren. Werner Burkhardt, geb..6.11.06, 1.SS-Pz.Gren.Ers.Btl.
SS-Pz.Gren. Walter Schmidt, geb. 13.7.21, 1.SS-Pz.Gren.Ers.Btl.
SS-Rttf. Fritz Krenzke, geb. 1.11.12, SS-Kav.-Ers.-Abt.

SS-Scharf. Nieratschker, Hugo, geb.18.6.09, Sicherheitspolizei

am 27.4.43 SS-Pz.Gren. Friedrich Czwielung, geb.5.4.07, 1.SS-Pz.Gren.E.B.
SS-Pz.Gren. Heinrich Meyer, geb. 16.10.10, 1.SS-Pz.Gren.Ers.Btl.

Gruppen-Wm. Jurko Kosatschok, geb.3.5.21, Ausb.L. Trawniki

poln. Pol.Wm. Boleslaw Stasik, geb.18.9.10, 8. Komm.

am 28.4.43 SS-Strm. Hans Petry, geb. 10.4.23, 1.SS-Pz.Gren.Ers.Btl.
SS-Uscha. Erich Schulz, geb. 25.1.24, 2.SS-Pz.Gren.Ers.Btl.

Wm.d.Schp.d.R. Oskar Hexel, geb. 15.2.17, III/SS-Pol. 22

SS Technical Sergeant Sepp Mayowski, born 23 December 1914, Trawniki Training Camp

Polish Police Sergeant Boleslaw Gruschecki, born 1 June 1914, Field and Guard Division

On 21 April 1943

SS Trooper Johann Lebisch, born 6 June 1921, Cavalry Reserve Division

Train Guard of the Protective Police Kurt Szesnik, born 9 November 1909, SS Police Regiment No. 22, 3d Battalion

Train Sergeant of the Protective Police Erich Paerschke, born 30 December 1914, SS Police Regiment No. 22, 1st Battalion

Guard Iwan Knyhynyzkyj, born 21 July 1923, Trawniki Training Camp

On 22 April 1943

Train Sergeant of the Protective Police Otto Koglin, born 3 April 1911, SS Police Regiment No. 22, 1st Battalion

On 23 April 1943

Train Sergeant of the Protective Police Erich Waclawik, born 25 April 1910, SS Police Regiment No. 22, 3d Battalion

Sergeant of the Protective Police Reserves Karl Neidhard, born 14 March 1903, SS Police Regiment No. 22, 3d Battalion

Guard Emil Schmidt, born 2 February 1923, Trawniki Training Camp

On 24 April 1943

SS Sergeant Franz Luedke, born 22 October 1922, 1st SS Panzer Grenadier Reserve Battalion

SS Panzer Grenadier Siegfried Boeckmann, born 14 October 1912, 1st SS Panzer Grenadier Reserve Battalion

Unit Guard Wladimir Usik, born 16 June 1917, Trawniki Training Camp

On 25 April 1943

SS Panzer Grenadier Werner Burkhardt, born 6 November 1906, 1st SS Panzer Grenadier Reserve Battalion

SS Panzer Grenadier Walter Schmidt, born 13 July 1921, 1st SS Panzer Grenadier Reserve Battalion

SS Corporal Fritz Krenzke, born 1 November 1912, SS Cavalry Reserve Division

SS Staff Sergeant Hugo Nieratschker, born 18 June 1909, Security Police

On 27 April 1943

SS Panzer Grenadier Friedrich Czwielung, born 5 April 1907, 1st SS Panzer Grenadier Reserve Battalion

SS Panzer Grenadier Heinrich Meyer, born 16 October 1910, 1st SS Panzer Grenadier Reserve Battalion

Unit Guard Jurko Kosatschok, born 3 May 1921, Trawniki Training Camp

Polish Police Sergeant Boleslaw Stasik, born 18 September 1910, 8th Commissariat

On 28 April 1943

SS Private First Class Hans Petry, born 10 April 1923, 1st SS Panzer Grenadier Reserve Battalion

SS Sergeant Erich Schulz, born 25 January 1924, 2nd SS Panzer Grenadier Reserve Battalion

Sergeant of the Protective Police Oskar Hexel, born 15 February 1917, SS Police Regiment No. 22, 3d Battalion

am 1.5.43　poln.Pol.-Anw. Jerzy Mostowski, geb.21.1.20, Gel.u.Wach-Abt.
　　　　　poln. Pol.Wm. Antoni Gladkowski,geb.21.1.04　Gel.u.Wach-Abt.

am 2.5.43　Obw.d.Schp. Robert Linke, geb. 6.3.09, III/SS-Pol. 22

am 3.5.43　SS-Pz.Gren. Clemens Kapitza, geb.22.11.24, 1.SS-Pz.Gren.Ers.Btl.
　　　　　SS-Reiter Georg Pöppl, geb. 18.1.24, SS-Kav.-Ers.-Abt.
　　　　　SS-Schütze Andreas Kuding, geb. 25.1.24, SS-Kav.-Ers.-Abt.

am 5.5.43　SS-Rttf. Fritz Wiek, geb. 15.8.21, SS-Kav.-Ers.-Abt.

am 6.5.43　SS-Uscha. Hans Forster, geb. 31.5.14, 2.SS-Pz.Gren.Ers.Btl.

am 7.5.43　SS-Reiter Ludwig Török, geb. 8.9.24, SS-Kav.-Ers.-Abt.

am 8.5.43　SS-Uscha. Fritz Vogel, geb. 31.10.20, SS-Kav.-Ers.-Abt.
　　　　　SS-Uscha. Robert Hauschild, geb. 19.3.21, SS-Kav.-Ers.-Abt.

　　　　　Schütze Otto Kiel, geb. 17.4.24, Eisenb.Pz.E-Abt.Pi-Kdo.
　　　　　　　　　　　　　　　　　　　　Rembertow

am 10.5.43　SS-Mann Johann Nieszner, geb. 23.4.22, SS-Kav.-Ers.-Abt.
　　　　　　SS-Mann Hermann Herbst, geb. 26.4.25, SS-Kav.-Ers.-Abt.
　　　　　　SS-Mann Rudolf Hörnicke, geb. 27.8.25, SS-Kav.-Ers.-Abt.
　　　　　　SS-Reiter Anton Heit, geb. 17.9.21, SS-Kav.-Ers.-Abt.

am 11.5.43　SS-Uscha. Hugo Mielke, geb. 9.6.12, SS-Kav.-Ers.-Abt.
　　　　　　SS-Reiter Werner Erbes, geb. 24.5.24, SS-Kav.-Ers.-Abt.

am 12.5.43　SS-Rttf. Josef Schuster, geb. 15.3.20, SS-Kav.-Ers.-Abt.

am 13.5.43　SS-Schütze Johann Barlock, geb.24.12.23,SS-Kav.-Ers.-Abt.
　　　　　　SS-Pz.Gren. Otto Döppe, geb. 1.11.24, 3. SS-Pz.Gren.Ers.Btl.
　　　　　　SS-Pz.Gren. Franz Kosarz, geb. 6.1.24, 3.SS-Pz.Gren.Ers.Btl.
　　　　　　SS-Pz.Gren. Alfred Baldt, geb.15.9.06, 5.SS-Pz.Gren.Ers.Btl.

On 1 May 1943
 Polish Police Private Jerzy Mostowski, born 21 January 1920, Field and
  Guard Division
 Polish Police Sergeant Antoni Gladkowski, born 21 January 1904, Field
  and Guard Division

On 2 May 1943
 Staff Sergeant of the Protective Police Robert Linke, born 6 March 1909,
  SS Police Regiment No. 22, 3d Battalion

On 3 May 1943
 SS Panzer Grenadier Clemens Kapitza, born 22 November 1924, 1st SS
  Panzer Grenadier Reserve Battalion
 SS Trooper Georg Poeppl, born 18 January 1924, SS Cavalry Reserve Division
 SS Private Andreas Kuding, born 25 January 1924, SS Cavalry Reserve Division

On 5 May 1943
 SS Corporal Fritz Wiek, born 15 August 1921, SS Cavalry Reserve Division

On 6 May 1943
 SS Sergeant Hans Forster, born 31 May 1914, 2nd SS Panzer Grenadier
  Reserve Battalion

On 7 May 1943
 SS Trooper Ludwig Toeroek, born 8 September 1924, SS Cavalry Reserve Division

On 8 May 1943
 SS Sergeant Fritz Vogel, born 31 October 1920, SS Cavalry Reserve Division
 SS Sergeant Robert Hauschild, born 19 March 1921, SS Calavry Reserve Division
 Private Otto Kiel, born 17 April 1924, Engineers Detail of the Railway
  Armored Trains—Reserve Division Rembertow

On 10 May 1943
 SS Private Johann Nieszner, born 23 April 1922, SS Cavalry Reserve Division
 SS Private Hermann Herbst, born 26 April 1925, SS Cavalry Reserve Division
 SS Private Rudolf Hoernicke, born 27 August 1925, SS Cavalry Reserve Division
 SS Trooper Anton Heit, born 17 September 1921, SS Cavalry Reserve Division

On 11 May 1943
 SS Sergeant Hugo Mielke, born 9 June 1912, SS Cavalry Reserve Division
 SS Trooper Werner Erbes, born 24 May 1924, SS Cavalry Reserve Division

On 12 May 1943
 SS Corporal Josef Schuster, born 15 March 1920, SS Cavalry Reserve Division

On 13 May 1943
 SS Private Johann Barlock, born 24 December 1923, SS Cavalry Reserve Division
 SS Panzer Grenadier Otto Doeppe, born 1 November 1924, 3d SS Panzer
  Grenadier Reserve Battalion
 SS Panzer Grenadier Frank Kosarz, born 6 January 1924, 3d SS Panzer
  Grenadier Reserve Battalion
 SS Panzer Grenadier Alfred Baldt, born 15 September 1906, 5th SS Panzer
  Grenadier Reserve Battalion

am 14.5.43   ⁜-Oscha. Thomas Wachter, geb.12.2.19, 4.⁜-Pz.Gren.Ers.Btl.
             ⁜-Rttf. Josef Posch, geb. 22.7.20, 4. ⁜-Pz.Gren.Ers.Batl.
             ⁜-Uscha. Martin Enzbrunner, geb.19.1.22, 4.⁜-Pz.Gren.E.B.
             ⁜-Pz.Gren.Hans Räder, geb. 10.10.16, 4. ⁜-Pz.Gren.Ers.Btl.
             Zugwm.d.Schp. Alfons Czapp, geb.15.9.11, I/⁜-Pol. 22

am 15.5.43   Wm.d.Schp.d.R. Otto Luenen, geb.19.12.05, III/⁜-Pol. 23

On 14 May 1943

SS Technical Sergeant Thomas Wachter, born 12 February 1919, 4th SS Panzer Grenadier Reserve Battalion

SS Corporal Josef Posch, born 22 July 1920, 4th SS Panzer Grenadier Reserve Battalion

SS Sergeant Martin Enzbrunner, born 19 January 1922, 4th SS Panzer Grenadier Reserve Battalion

SS Panzer Grenadier Hans Raeder, born 10 October 1916, 4th SS Panzer Grenadier Reserve Battalion

Train Sergeant of the Protective Police Alfons Czapp, born 15 September 1911, SS Police Regiment No. 22, 1st Battalion

On 15 May 1943

Sergeant of the Protective Police Reserves Otto Luenen, born 19 December 1905, SS Police Regiment No. 23, 3d Battalion

Einsatzkräfte

=================================

                                                    Durchschnitts-
                                                    Tageseinsatz

Waffen-ᚦᚦ:

ᚦᚦ-Pz.Gren.Ausb.u.Ers.Btl. 3 Warschau   4/440
ᚦᚦ-Kav.-Ausb.-u.Ers.-Abt. Warschau   5/381

Ordnungspolizei:
   ᚦᚦ-Pol.-Rgt. 22, I. Btl.   3/94
                III. Btl.   3/134
   Technische Nothilfe   1/6
   poln. Polizei   4/363
   poln. Feuerlöschpolizei   166

Sicherheitspolizei: 3/32

Wehrmacht

Leichte Flakalarmbatterie III/8 Warschau   2/22
Pionierkommando d. Eisenb.Panzerzug-
Ers.-Abt. Rembertow   2/42
Res.-Pionier-Btl. 14 Gora-Kalwaria   1/34

Fremdvölkische Wachmannschaften:

1 Batl. Trawnikimänner   2/335

Forces Used*

	Average number of personnel used per day
Waffen-SS	
SS Panzer Grenadier Training and Reserve Battalion No. 3, Warsaw	4 officers/440 men
SS Cavalry Training and Reserve Division, Warsaw	5 officers/381 men
Order Police[2]	
SS Police Regiment No. 22 1st Battalion	3 officers/ 94 men
SS Police Regiment No. 22, 3d Battalion	3 officers/134 men
Technical Emergency Corps	1 officer / 6 men
Polish Police	4 officers/363 men
Polish Fire Brigade	166 men
Security Police	3 officers/ 32 men
Wehrmacht (Armed Forces)	
Light Anti-aircraft Alarm Battery No. III/8, Warsaw	2 officers/ 22 men
Engineers Detail of the Railway Armored Trains—Reserve Division Rembertow	2 officers/ 42 men
Reserve Engineer Battalion No. 14, Gora-Kalwaria	1 officer / 34 men
Foreign Ethnic Units	
1 Battalion Trawniki Men[3]	2 officers/335 men

* The reader will note that the lists of dead and wounded contain references to units not listed under *Forces Used*.

I

Die Bildung jüdischer Wohnbezirke und die Auferlegung von Aufenthalts- und Wirtschaftsbeschränkungen für die Juden sind in der Geschichte des Ostens nicht neu. Ihre Anfänge gehen weit bis ins Mittelalter zurück und waren auch noch im Verlaufe der letzten Jahrhunderte immer wieder zu beobachten. Diese Beschränkungen erfolgten aus dem Gesichtspunkte, die arische Bevölkerung vor den Juden zu schützen.

Aus den gleichen Erwägungen wurde bereits im Februar 1940 der Gedanke der Bildung eines jüdischen Wohnbezirks in Warschau aufgegriffen. Es war zunächst geplant, den durch die Weichsel östlich abgegrenzten Stadtteil Warschaus zum jüdischen Wohnbezirk zu machen. Bei den besonders gelagerten Verhältnissen der Stadt Warschau mutete dieser Gedanke zunächst als undurchführbar an. Es wurden auch Einwände gegen diesen Plan von verschiedenen Seiten, insbesondere von der Stadtverwaltung, geltend gemacht. Man berief sich insbesondere darauf, daß die Errichtung eines jüdischen Wohnbezirkes erhebliche Störungen in der Industrie und Wirtschaft hervorrufen würde und daß eine Ernährung der in einem geschlossenen Wohnbezirk zusammengefaßten Juden nicht möglich sei.

Auf Grund einer im März 1940 erfolgten Besprechung wurde der Plan einer Ghettobildung mit Rücksicht auf die vorgetragenen Bedenken vorerst zurückgestellt. Zur gleichen Zeit wurde der Gedanke erwogen, den Distrikt Lublin zum Sammelbecken aller Juden des Generalgouvernements, insbesondere der aus dem Reich eintreffenden evakuierten Juden und Judenflüchtlinge, zu erklären. Aber schon im April 1940 wurde vom Höheren ⚡- und Polizeiführer Ost, Krakau, mitgeteilt, daß eine solche Zusammenfassung der Juden im Distrikt Lublin nicht beabsichtigt sei.

In der Zwischenzeit häuften sich eigenmächtige und unberechtigte Grenzübertritte von Juden. Insbesondere war dies an der Grenze der Kreishauptmannschaften Lowitsch und Skierniewice festzustel-

I

The creation of Jewish quarters and the imposition of residential and economic restrictions on the Jews are nothing new in the history of the East. These practices began as far back as the Middle Ages and have continued through the last few centuries. These restrictions were imposed with the intention of protecting the Aryan population from the Jews.

By February 1940, the same considerations led to the idea of creating a Jewish quarter in Warsaw. The original plan called for the establishment of a Jewish quarter in the part of Warsaw that is bounded on the east by the Vistula River. The situation prevailing in the city of Warsaw at first seemed to make this plan unworkable. There were also objections from various parties, especially from the city administration, which claimed that the establishment of a Jewish quarter would cause extensive disruptions in industry and the economy, and that it would be impossible to assure food supplies for Jews who were concentrated in an enclosed quarter.

Due to these objections, the plan to create a Ghetto was set aside at a conference in March 1940. At the same time, consideration was given to making the Lublin District a reservation for all Jews in the General Government [*Generalgouvernement*], particularly for evacuated and fleeing Jews arriving from the Reich. But the Higher SS and Police Leader East in Cracow informed us in April 1940 that such a concentration of Jews in the Lublin District was not intended.

In the interim, the number of arbitrary and unwarranted frontier crossings by Jews increased. This was especially true at the border of the Lowicz and Skierniewice districts. These illegal migrations of Jews began to threaten not

len. Die Verhältnisse der Stadt Lowitsch wurden durch diese illegalen Judenzuwanderungen sowohl in hygienischer als auch in sicherheitspolizeilicher Hinsicht bedrohlich. Der Kreishauptmann in Lowitsch ging deshalb, um diese Gefahren abzuwehren, dazu über,in seinem Kreise jüdische Wohnbezirke zu bilden.

Die Erfahrungen, die mit der Errichtung der jüdischen Wohnbezirke im Kreise Lowitsch gemacht wurden, zeigten, daß diese Methoden die einzig richtigen sind, um die Gefahren zu bannen, die von den Juden immer wieder ausgingen.

Die Errichtung eines jüdischen Wohnbezirkes auch in der Stadt Warschau wurde im Sommer 1940 immer dringlicher, da nach der Beendigung des Frankreichfeldzuges im Raume des Distrikts Warschau immer mehr Truppen zusammengezogen wurden. Von der Abteilung Gesundheitswesen wurde damals die Errichtung eines jüdischen Wohnbezirks im Interesse der Erhaltung der Gesundheit der deutschen Truppen und auch der Bevölkerung als besonders dringlich dargestellt. Die ursprünglich im Februar 1940 vorgesehene Errichtung eines jüdischen Wohnbezirks in der Vorstadt Praga hätte mit Rücksicht auf die Umgruppierung von nahezu 600 000 Menschen mindestens 4 bis 5 Monate in Anspruch genommen.Da aber in den Wintermonaten erfahrungsgemäß mit einem starken Auftreten der Seuchen zu rechnen war und aus diesem Grunde nach den Darlegungen des Distriktsarztes die Umsiedlungsaktion bis spätestens 15.11.1940 durchgeführt werden mußte, ließ man den Plan eines Stadtrandghettos in Praga fallen und wählte dafür als Raum für den neu zu bildenden jüdischen Wohnbezirk das bisher vorhandene Seuchensperrgebiet in der Stadt aus. Im Oktober 1940 wies der Gouverneur den Beauftragten des Distriktschefs für die Stadt Warschau an, bis zum 15.11.1940 die zur Bildung des jüdischen Wohnbezirks in der Stadt Warschau erforderlichen Umsiedlungen durchzuführen.

Der so gebildete jüdische Wohnbezirk in der Stadt Warschau wurde von etwa 400 000 Juden bewohnt. Es befanden sich in ihm 27 000 Wohnungen mit einem Zimmerdurchschnitt von 2 1/2 Zimmern. Er war

only hygienic but also security conditions in the town of Lowicz. In order to avert these dangers, the senior district official began to create Jewish quarters in his district.

The experiences derived from the establishment of Jewish quarters in the Lowicz District showed that these methods were the only suitable ones to banish the dangers which emanate from the Jews.

The need to create a Jewish quarter in the city of Warsaw as well became more and more pressing in the summer of 1940, when, with the end of the French campaign, even larger numbers of troops assembled in the district of Warsaw. At this point, the Department of Health strongly urged the establishment of a Jewish quarter in order to preserve the health of the German troops as well as that of the civilian population. Considering that a regroupment of almost 600,000 people was required, implementation of the original plan of February 1940 to establish a Jewish quarter in the suburb of Praga would have taken four to five months. Since experience indicated that a high incidence of epidemics could be expected in the winter months, the plan for a suburban Ghetto in Praga was dropped; and the city's quarantine district was chosen instead for use as a Jewish quarter. On the advice of the district medical officer, resettlement had to be completed by 15 November 1940 at the latest. The Governor ordered the plenipotentiary of the Warsaw District Chief to complete the resettlements necessary to the creation of a Jewish quarter within the city of Warsaw by this date.

About 400,000 Jews lived in this Jewish quarter. It contained 27,000 apartments, averaging 2½ rooms. It was separated from the rest of the city

von dem übrigen Stadtgebiet durch Brand- und Trennmauern und
durch Vermauerung von Straßenzügen, Fenstern, Türen, Baulücken
abgetrennt.

Die Verwaltung des neugebildeten jüdischen Wohnbezirkes lag in
Händen des jüdischen Ältestenrates, der seine Weisungen von dem
dem Gouverneur direkt unterstellten Kommissar für den jüdischen
Wohnbezirk empfing. Die Juden hatten eine Selbstverwaltung, an
der die deutsche Aufsicht nur insoweit Interesse nahm, als deutsche Belange berührt wurden. Zur wirksamen Durchführung der vom
jüdischen Ältestenrat zu ergreifenden Maßnahmen wurde ein jüdischer Ordnungsdienst eingerichtet, der durch besondere Armbinde
und Mütze gekennzeichnet und mit Gummiknüppeln ausgerüstet war.
Dieser jüdische Ordnungsdienst hatte die Aufgabe, für die Ord-
nung und Sicherheit innerhalb des jüdischen Wohnbezirkes zu sor-
gen und unterstand der deutschen und polnischen Polizei.

                              II

Schon bald stellte es sich heraus, daß trotz dieser Zusammenballung der Juden nicht alle Gefahren gebannt waren. Die Sicher-
heitslage machte es erforderlich, die Juden aus der Stadt Warschau
ganz herauszunehmen. Die erste große Aussiedlung fand in der Zeit
vom 22. Juli bis 3. Oktober 1942 statt. Es wurden hierbei 310 322
Juden ausgesiedelt. Im Januar 1943 erfolgte abermals eine Umsiedlungsaktion, mit welcher insgesamt 6 500 Juden erfaßt wurden.

Im Januar 1943 wurde vom Reichsführer-ϟϟ anläßlich seines Besuches
in Warschau dem ϟϟ- und Polizeiführer im Distrikt Warschau der Befehl erteilt, die im Ghetto untergebrachten Rüstungs- und wehr-
wirtschaftlichen Betriebe mit Arbeitskräften und Maschinen nach
Lublin zu verlagern. Die Durchführung dieses Befehls gestaltete
sich recht schwierig, da sowohl die Betriebsführer als auch die
Juden dieser Verlagerung sich in jeder denkbaren Weise wider-
setzten. Der ϟϟ- und Polizeiführer entschloß sich deshalb, durch

by fire and partition walls and by walled-up thoroughfares, windows, doors, and empty lots.

The Jewish Council [*Aeltestenrat*] administered the new Jewish quarter.[4] It received its instructions from the Commissioner for the Jewish quarter, who was directly subordinate to the Governor. The Jews had administrative autonomy, and German supervision was limited to occasions when German interests were affected. A Jewish Police [*Ordnungsdienst*] was established to implement orders of the Jewish Council. They were identified by special arm bands and caps, and were armed with rubber truncheons. This Jewish police force was responsible for maintaining order and security within the Jewish quarter and was subordinate to the German and Polish Police.

II

It soon became clear that not all dangers had been banished by confining the Jews to one district. Security considerations necessitated that Jews be completely removed from the city of Warsaw. The first large removal occurred during the period from 22 July to 3 October 1942, when 310,322 Jews were removed.[5] In January 1943, another resettlement operation was carried out, which encompassed a total of 6,500 Jews.[6]

On the occasion of his visit to Warsaw in January 1943, the Reichsfuehrer-SS ordered the SS and Police Leader of the Warsaw District *to transfer from the Ghetto to Lublin all armament and defense industries inclusive of their work force and machines.* The implementation of this command proved to be very difficult, since the managers as well as the Jews resisted in every conceivable way. Therefore, the SS and Police Leader decided that a forced

- 4 -

eine für 3 Tage vorgesehene Großaktion die Verlagerung der Betriebe zwangsweise durchzuführen. Die Vorbereitungen und der
Einsatzbefehl für diese Großaktion waren von meinem Vorgänger
getroffen worden. Ich selbst traf am 17. April 1943 in Warschau
ein und übernahm die Führung der Großaktion am 19.4.1943 um
8.00 Uhr, nachdem die Aktion selbst schon um 6.00 Uhr an diesem
Tage begonnen hatte.

Vor dem Beginn dieser Großaktion waren die Grenzen des ehemaligen jüdischen Wohnbezirkes durch eine äußere Absperrung abgeriegelt, um einen Ausbruch der Juden zu vermeiden. Diese Absperrung
bestand fortlaufend vom Beginn bis zum Ende der Aktion und war
nachts noch besonders verstärkt.

Beim ersten Eindringen in das Ghetto gelang es den Juden und den
polnischen Banditen, durch einen vorbereiteten Feuerüberfall die
angesetzten Kräfte einschließlich Panzer- und Schützenpanzerwa-
gen zurückzuschlagen. Bei dem zweiten Einsatz, etwa gegen 8.00
Uhr, setzte ich die Kräfte getrennt durch bekanntgegebene Ge-
fechtsstreifen truppenmäßig zur Durchkämmung des gesamten Ghettos
an. Trotz Wiederholung des Feuerüberfalles gelang es jetzt, die
Gebäudekomplexe planmäßig zu durchkämmen. Der Gegner wurde ge -
zwungen, sich von den Dächern und höher gelegenen Stützpunkten
in die Keller, Bunker und Kanäle zurückzuziehen. Um ein Entwei -
chen in die Kanalisation zu verhindern, wurde alsbald das Kanalnetz unterhalb des jüdischen Wohnbezirkes mit Wasser angestaut,
was aber von den Juden zum größten Teil durch Sprengungen von Ab-
sperrschiebern illusorisch gemacht wurde. Am Abend des ersten Tages wurde auf größeren Widerstand gestoßen, der aber von einer
besonders angesetzten Kampfgruppe rasch gebrochen werden konnte.
Beim weiteren Einsatz gelang es, die Juden aus ihren eingerichteten Widerstandsnestern, Schützenlöchern usw. zu vertreiben und im
Laufe des 20. und 21. April den größten Teil des sogen. Restghettos soweit in die Hand zu bekommen, daß von einem größeren erheblichen Widerstand innerhalb dieser Gebäudekomplexe nicht mehr ge-
sprochen werden konnte.

transfer be carried out by means of a three-day grand operation [*Grossaktion*]. The preparation and combat orders for the grand operation were initiated by my predecessor. I arrived in Warsaw on 17 April 1943 and took command of the grand operation on 19 April 1943 at 0800 hours. The operation had already started the same day at 0600 hours.

To prevent the Jews from escaping, the borders of the former Jewish quarter were secured from the outside by a barricade before the start of the grand operation. This barricade was maintained from start to finish of the operation and was reinforced at night.

The Jews and Polish bandits[7] succeeded in repelling the first penetration of the Ghetto by ambushing the participating units, which included tanks and armored cars. During the second attack, at about 0800 hours, I committed the attack units to various predetermined battle sectors with orders to sweep the entire Ghetto. Despite a second ambush, the blocks of buildings were swept according to plan. The enemy was forced to withdraw from roofs and from strongholds above ground level into basements, bunkers, and sewers. The sewer system was dammed up below the Jewish quarter and flooded to prevent escape into the sewers. Most of this plan, however, proved illusory when the Jews blew up the cutoff valves. Heavy resistance was encountered on the first evening but was quickly broken by a special battle unit. During further operations, the Jews were driven out of their furnished nests of resistance, sniper holes, etc. During 20 and 21 April, the greater part of the so-called remnant Ghetto* came under our control, and resistance within these blocks could no longer be termed very substantial.

*See map for the location and a description of the remnant Ghetto.

- 5 -

Die Hauptkampfgruppe der Juden, die mit polnischen Banditen ver-
mengt war, zog sich schon im Laufe des 1. bzw. 2. Tages auf den
sogen. Muranowskiplatz zurück. Dort war sie von einer größeren
Anzahl polnischer Banditen verstärkt worden. Sie hatte den Plan,
mit allen Mitteln sich im Ghetto festzusetzen, um ein Eindringen
unsererseits zu verhindern. Es wurden die jüdische und die pol -
nische Flagge als Aufruf zum Kampf gegen uns auf einem Betonhaus
gehißt. Diese beiden Fahnen konnten aber schon am zweiten Tage
des Einsatzes von einer besonderen Kampfgruppe erbeutet werden.
Bei diesem Feuerkampf mit den Banditen fiel ⚡-Untersturmführer
D e h m k e , indem eine von ihm in der Hand gehaltene Handgrana-
te durch feindlichen Beschuß zur Explosion kam und ihn tödlich
verletzte.

Schon bald nach den ersten Tagen erkannte ich, daß der ursprünglich vorgesehene Plan nicht zur Durchführung zu bringen war, wenn
die überall im Ghetto verteilt liegenden Rüstungs- und Wehrwirt-
schaftsbetriebe nicht aufgelöst würden. Es war deshalb notwendig,
diese Betriebe unter Ansetzung eines angemessenen Termins zur
Räumung und sofortigen Verlagerung aufzufordern. So wurde ein Betrieb nach dem anderen behandelt und dadurch in kürzester Frist
erreicht, daß die den Juden und Banditen sich bietende Möglichkeit, immer wieder in diese von der Wehrmacht betreuten Betriebe
hinüberzuwechseln, genommen wurde. Um entscheiden zu können, in
welcher Zeit diese Betriebe geräumt werden konnten, waren einge-
hende Besichtigungen notwendig. Die bei diesen Besichtigungen
festgestellten Zustände sind unbeschreiblich. Ich kann mir nicht
vorstellen, daß irgendwo anders ein größerer Wirrwarr bestanden
haben kann als in dem Warschauer Ghetto. Die Juden hatten alles
in ihren Händen, von chemischen Mitteln zur Anfertigung von
Sprengstoffen angefangen bis zu Bekleidungs- und Ausrüstungs -
stücken der Wehrmacht. Die Betriebsführer hatten in ihren Betrieben so wenig Übersicht, daß es den Juden möglich war, innerhalb
dieser Betriebe Kampfmittel aller Art, insbesondere Wurfgranaten
und Molotow-Cocktails usw. herzustellen.

Ferner ist es den Juden gelungen, in diesen Betrieben Wider -

The main Jewish fighting unit, which was intermingled with Polish bandits, had already withdrawn during the first or second day to the so-called Muranowski Square. They were reinforced there by a considerable number of Polish bandits. Their plan was to entrench themselves in the Ghetto by every means in order to prevent our penetration. The Jewish and Polish flags were hoisted on top of a concrete building in a call to battle against us. But both flags became the booty of a special battle unit on the second day of the engagement. During this skirmish with the bandits, SS Second Lieutenant Dehmke was killed when the hand grenade he held was triggered by enemy fire, exploded, and injured him fatally.

After the first few days, I realized that the original plan could not be carried out without dissolving the armament and military enterprises that were located throughout the Ghetto. It was therefore necessary to set a suitable deadline and to request these enterprises to proceed with an evacuation and immediate transfer. One firm after another was dealt with in this way, and Jews and bandits were quickly deprived of the opportunity to relocate to those enterprises supervised by the Wehrmacht. Thorough inspections were necessary in order to decide how much time was needed to evacuate these enterprises. The conditions discovered during these inspections are indescribable. I cannot imagine another place as chaotic as the Warsaw Ghetto. The Jews controlled everything, from chemical substances used in the manufacture of explosives to items of clothing and equipment for the Wehrmacht. The managers oversaw their operations so poorly that it was possible for the Jews to produce all kinds of weapons, especially hand grenades, Molotov cocktails, etc.

Furthermore, the Jews succeeded in establishing pockets of resistance in

standsnester einzurichten. Ein derartiges Widerstandsnest mußte
bereits am zweiten Tag in einem Betrieb der Heeresunterkunfts -
verwaltung durch Einsatz eines Pionierzuges mit Flammenwerfern
und Artilleriebeschuß bekämpft werden. Die Juden hatten sich in
diesem Betrieb derartig eingenistet, daß es nicht möglich war,
sie zum freiwilligen Verlassen der Betriebsstätte zu bewegen,wes-
halb ich mich entschloß, den Betrieb am nächsten Tage durch Feuer zu vernichten.

Die Betriebsführer dieser Betriebe, die meistens von einem Offi-
zier der Wehrmacht noch betreut wurden, waren in fast allen Fällen nicht in der Lage, konkrete Angaben über die Bestände und
den Ort der Lagerung dieser Bestände zu machen. Die von ihnen gemachten Angaben über die Zahl der bei ihnen beschäftigten Juden
stimmte in keinem Falle. Es mußte immer wieder festgestellt werden, daß in diesen Häuserlabyrinthen, die als Wohnblocks zu den
Rüstungsbetrieben gehörten, reiche Juden unter dem Deckmantel
eines Rüstungsarbeiters mit ihren Familien Unterkunft gefunden
hatten und dort ein herrliches Leben führten. Trotz aller ergan-
genen Befehle, die Juden zum Verlassen der Betriebe aufzufordern,
mußte mehrfach festgestellt werden, daß Betriebsführer die Juden
in der Erwartung einschlossen, daß die Aktion nur wenige Tage
dauern würde, um dann mit den ihnen verbleibenden Juden weiter-
zuarbeiten. Nach Aussagen festgenommener Juden sollen Firmenin-
haber mit Juden Zechgelage veranstaltet haben. Hierbei sollen
auch Frauen eine große Rolle gespielt haben. Die Juden sollen be-
strebt gewesen sein, mit Offizieren und Männern der Wehrmacht guten Verkehr zu unterhalten. Es seien öfters Zechgelage vorgekommen und im Laufe derselben zwischen Deutschen und Juden gemeinsa-
me Geschäfte getätigt worden.

Die Zahl der in den ersten Tagen aus den Häusern herausgeholten
und erfaßten Juden war verhältnismäßig gering. Es zeigte sich,
daß sich die Juden in den Kanälen und besonders eingerichteten
Bunkern versteckt hielten. Wenn in den ersten Tagen angenommen
worden war, daß nur vereinzelte Bunker vorhanden seien, so zeig-

these enterprises. One such place, located in a plant under the jurisdiction of the Quartermaster's office, had to be attacked as early as the second day of operations by an Engineers' unit, equipped with flame throwers and artillery. The Jews were so entrenched in this enterprise that it was not possible to induce them to leave voluntarily. I therefore resolved to destroy this enterprise by fire the next day.

In almost all instances, the plant managers, who were usually still supervised by a Wehrmacht officer, were not able to provide precise data about their stocks and storage locations. Their declarations about the number of Jews in their employ were incorrect in every case. Repeatedly, it was discovered that in these labyrinths of buildings, which served as housing blocks of the armament plants, rich Jews disguised as defense workers had found accommodations for themselves and their families and were leading magnificent lives. Despite all orders to request the Jews to leave the enterprises, it was frequently discovered that managers simply included the Jews in their expectation that the operation would last only a few days, after which they expected to continue work with the remaining Jews. According to statements by arrested Jews, owners of enterprises were said to have gone on drinking sprees with Jews. Women allegedly played a prominent part in this. It was said that Jews endeavored to keep up good relations with officers and men of the Wehrmacht. Business deals are said to have been concluded between Jews and Germans during frequent drinking sprees.

The number of Jews who were removed from houses and apprehended was relatively small during the first days. It was apparent that the Jews were hiding in sewers and specially constructed bunkers. During the first days, it was assumed that there were only scattered bunkers. However, during the grand operation, the whole Ghetto was found to be systematically equipped

te sich doch im Laufe der Großaktion, daß das ganze Ghetto systematisch mit Kellern, Bunkern und Gängen versehen war. Diese Gänge und Bunker hatten in allen Fällen Zugänge zu der Kanalisation.
Dadurch war ein ungestörter Verkehr unter der Erde zwischen den
Juden möglich. Dieses Kanalnetz benutzten die Juden auch dazu,um
unter der Erde in den arischen Teil der Stadt Warschau zu ent -
kommen. Laufend trafen Meldungen ein, daß Juden sich durch die
Kanallöcher zu entziehen versuchten. Unter dem Vorwand, Luft -
schutzkeller zu bauen, wurden seit dem Spätherbst 1942 in diesem
ehemaligen jüdischen Wohnbezirk die Bunker errichtet. Sie sollten
dazu dienen, sämtliche Juden bei der schon lange vermuteten neuen
Umsiedlung aufzunehmen und von hier aus den Widerstand gegen die
Einsatzkräfte zu organisieren. Durch Maueranschläge, Flugzettel
und Flüsterpropaganda hatte die kommunistische Widerstandsbewe-
gung im ehemaligen jüdischen Wohnbezirk auch erreicht, daß mit Beginn der neuen Großaktion die Bunker sofort bezogen wurden. Wie
vorsorglich die Juden gearbeitet hatten, beweist die in vielen Fällen festgestellte geschickte Anlage der Bunker mit Wohneinrichtun-
gen für ganze Familien, Wasch- und Badeeinrichtungen, Toilettenan-
lagen, Waffen- und Munitionskammern und großen Lebensmittelvorrä-
ten für mehrere Monate. Es gab besondere Bunker für arme und reiche Juden. Das Auffinden der einzelnen Bunker durch die Einsatzkräfte war infolge der Tarnung außerordentlich schwierig und in
vielen Fällen nur durch Verrat seitens der Juden möglich.

Schon nach den ersten Tagen stand fest, daß die Juden keinesfalls
mehr an eine freiwillige Umsiedlung dachten, sondern gewillt waren,
sich mit allen Möglichkeiten und den ihnen zur Verfügung stehenden Waffen zur Wehr zu setzen. Es hatten sich unter polnisch-bol-
schewistischer Führung sogen. Kampfgruppen gebildet, die bewaffnet waren und für die ihnen greifbaren Waffen jeden geforderten
Preis zahlten.

Während der Großaktion konnten Juden gefangen werden, die bereits
nach Lublin bzw. Treblinka verlagert waren, dort ausbrachen und

with cellars, bunkers, and passages. These bunkers and passages were all connected to the sewer system. Thus, the Jews were able to maintain an undisturbed subterranean traffic. They also used this sewer network to escape underground into the Aryan part of the city of Warsaw. Reports were continuously received that Jews attempted to get away through manholes. Under the pretext of building air-raid shelters, they had been constructing bunkers in the former Jewish quarter since late autumn 1942. The bunkers were intended to shelter the Jews during the new resettlement, which had long been anticipated, and to serve as their base of resistance against our troops. Using posters, leaflets, and word-of-mouth propaganda, the Communist resistance movement in the former Jewish quarter was able to man the bunkers occupied as soon as the new grand operation commenced. The skillful construction of the bunkers proved how providently the Jews had prepared themselves. The bunkers were furnished for entire families and equipped with washing and bathing facilities, toilets, storage rooms for arms and ammunition, and food supplies sufficient for several months. There were different bunkers for poor and rich Jews. Because of camouflage, the discovery of individual bunkers by the troops was extremely difficult. In many cases, discovery was possible only through betrayal by Jews.

After the first few days, it was clear that the Jews no longer considered voluntary resettlement but were determined to resist with all weapons and means at their disposal. So-called fighting groups had been formed under Polish-Bolshevik leadership. They were armed and paid any price for available weapons.

During the grand operation, Jews were caught who had already been transferred to Lublin or Treblinka, had escaped from there, and had returned to the

mit Waffen und Munition versehen in das Ghetto zurückkehrten.
Die polnischen Banditen fanden im Ghetto immer wieder Unter -
schlupf und blieben dort fast unbehelligt, weil keine Kräfte vorhanden waren, in diesen Wirrwarr einzudringen. Während es zu -
nächst möglich war, die an sich feigen Juden in größeren Massen
einzufangen, gestaltete sich die Erfassung der Banditen und Juden in der zweiten Hälfte der Großaktion immer schwieriger. Es
waren immer wieder Kampfgruppen von 20 bis 30 und mehr jüdischen
Burschen im Alter von 18 bis 25 Jahren, die jeweils eine entsprechende Anzahl Weiber bei sich hatten, die neuen Widerstand ent -
fachten. Diese Kampfgruppen hatten den Befehl, sich bis zum Letzten mit Waffengewalt zu verteidigen und sich gegebenenfalls der
Gefangennahme durch Selbstmord zu entziehen. Einer solchen Kampfgruppe gelang es, aus einem Siel der Kanalisation in der sogen.
Prosta einen Lastkraftwagen zu besteigen und damit zu entkommen
(etwa 30 bis 35 Banditen). Ein Bandit, der mit diesem Lastkraftwagen angekommen war, brachte 2 Handgranaten zur Entzündung, die
das Zeichen für die sich im Kanal bereithaltenden Banditen waren,
um aus dem Siel herauszuklettern. Die Banditen und Juden - es befanden sich darunter auch immer wieder polnische Banditen, die mit
Karabinern, Handfeuerwaffen und 1 lMG. bewaffnet waren - bestiegen den Lkw. und fuhren dann in unbekannter Richtung davon. Der
letzte Mann dieser Bande, der Wache im Kanal und den Auftrag hatte, den Deckel der Kanalöffnung zu schließen, wurde gefangen. Von
diesem stammen die vorstehend gemachten Angaben. Die angesetzte
Fahndung nach dem Lastkraftwagen ist leider ergebnislos verlaufen.

Bei dem bewaffneten Widerstand waren die zu den Kampfgruppen ge-
hörenden Weiber in gleicher Weise wie die Männer bewaffnet und
zum Teil Angehörige der Haluzzenbewegung. Es war keine Selten -
heit, daß diese Weiber aus beiden Händen mit Pistolen feuerten.
Immer wieder kam es vor, daß sie Pistolen und Handgranaten (polnische Eierhandgranaten) bis zum letzten Moment in ihren Schlüpfern verborgen hielten, um sie dann gegen die Männer der Waffen-#,
Polizei und Wehrmacht anzuwenden.

Ghetto, equipped with arms and ammunition. Polish bandits continually found refuge in the Ghetto and remained there almost unmolested, since no forces were available to penetrate this chaos. While it was possible at the beginning to catch considerable numbers of Jews, who are inherently cowardly, it proved increasingly difficult to capture Jews and bandits in the second half of the grand operation. Repeatedly, fighting groups of 20 to 30 or more Jewish youths, aged 18 to 25, accompanied by a corresponding number of females, unleashed new resistance. These fighting groups had orders to offer armed resistance to the last person and, if necessary, to commit suicide to escape capture. After ascending from a sewer opening in the so-called Prosta, one such fighting group (circa 30 to 35 bandits) succeeded in escaping in a truck. One bandit, who had arrived with this truck, exploded 2 hand grenades as a prearranged signal for the waiting bandits to emerge from the sewer. The Jews and bandits climbed into the truck and drove away in an unknown direction. These groups always included Polish bandits armed with carbines, small arms, and one light machine gun. The last member of the gang, who was on guard in the sewer and was assigned to replace the manhole cover, was captured. It was he who provided the above information. The search for the truck was unfortunately without result.

During the armed resistance, females belonging to fighting groups were armed just like the men. Some of them were members of the He-halutz movement.[8] Not infrequently, these females fired pistols from both hands. Repeatedly, they concealed pistols or hand grenades (oval Polish hand grenades) in their underpants to use at the last minute against the men of the Waffen-SS, Police, or Wehrmacht.

9

Der von den Juden und Banditen geleistete Widerstand konnte nur durch energischen, unermüdlichen Tag- und Nachteinsatz der Stoßtrupps gebrochen werden. Am 23.4.1943 erging vom Reichsführer-H über den Höheren H- und Polizeiführer Ost in Krakau der Befehl, die Durchkämmung des Ghettos in Warschau mit größter Härte und unnachsichtlicher Zähigkeit zu vollziehen. Ich entschloß mich deshalb, nunmehr die totale Vernichtung des jüdischen Wohnbezirks durch Abbrennen sämtlicher Wohnblocks, auch der Wohnblocks bei den Rüstungsbetrieben, vorzunehmen. Es wurde systematisch ein Betrieb nach dem anderen geräumt und anschließend durch Feuer vernichtet. Fast immer kamen dann die Juden aus ihren Verstecken und Bunkern heraus. Es war nicht selten, daß die Juden in den brennenden Häusern sich solange aufhielten, bis sie es wegen der Hitze und aus Angst vor dem Verbrennungstod vorzogen, aus den Stockwerken herauszuspringen, nachdem sie vorher Matratzen und andere Polstersachen aus den brennenden Häusern auf die Straße geworfen hatten. Mit gebrochenen Knochen versuchten sie dann noch über die Straße in Häuserblocks zu kriechen, die noch nicht oder nur teilweise in Flammen standen. Oft wechselten die Juden auch ihre Verstecke während der Nacht, indem sie sich in bereits abgebrannte Ruinen verzogen und dort solange Unterschlupf fanden, bis sie von den einzelnen Stoßtrupps aufgefunden wurden. Auch der Aufenthalt in den Kanälen war schon nach den ersten 8 Tagen kein angenehmer mehr. Häufig konnten auf der Straße durch die Schächte laute Stimmen aus den Kanälen herausgehört werden. Mutig kletterten dann die Männer der Waffen-H oder der Polizei oder Pioniere der Wehrmacht in die Schächte hinein, um die Juden herauszuholen und nicht selten stolperten sie dann über bereits verendete Juden oder wurden beschossen. Immer mußten Nebelkerzen in Anwendung gebracht werden, um die Juden herauszutreiben. So wurden an einem Tage 183 Kanaleinsteiglöcher geöffnet und in diese zu einer festgelegten X-Zeit Nebelkerzen herabgelassen mit dem Erfolg, daß die Banditen vor dem angeblichen Gas flüchtend im Zentrum des ehemaligen jüdischen Wohnbezirks zusammenliefen und aus den dort befindlichen Kanalöffnungen herausgeholt werden konnten. Zahlreiche Juden, die nicht gezählt werden konnten, wurden in Kanälen und Bunkern durch Sprengungen erledigt.

The resistance offered by the Jews and bandits could be broken only by the energetic and relentless day and night commitment of our assault units. *On 23 April 1943, the Reichsfuehrer-SS promulgated his order, transmitted through the Higher SS and Police Leader East in Cracow, to complete the sweeping of the Warsaw Ghetto with greatest severity and unrelenting tenacity.* I therefore decided to embark on the total destruction of the Jewish quarter by burning down every residential block, including the housing blocks belonging to the armament enterprises. One enterprise after another was systematically evacuated and destroyed by fire. In almost every instance, the Jews then emerged from their hiding places and bunkers. It was not unusual for Jews to remain in the burning houses until the heat and their fear of being cremated forced them to jump from the upper floors. They did so after throwing mattresses and other upholstered items into the street. With broken bones, they still tried to crawl across the street into housing blocks that had not yet been set on fire or were only partly in flames. Jews often changed their hiding places during the night, moving into already burned-out ruins and finding refuge there until they were found by one of our assault units. Nor was their stay in the sewers very pleasant after the first eight days. Frequently, the sewer shafts carried loud voices upward to the streets, whereupon men of the Waffen-SS, Police, or Wehrmacht Engineers courageously climbed down the shafts to bring out Jews. Not infrequently the Engineers would stumble over dead Jews or be shot at. It was always necessary to use smoke candles to drive out the Jews. On one day alone, at a predetermined hour, 183 sewer gates were opened and smoke candles lowered. The bandits fled from what they thought was gas toward the center of the former Jewish quarter, where they were pulled out of the sewer holes. An indeterminable number of Jews were finished off when sewers and bunkers were blown up.

10

Je länger der Widerstand andauerte, desto härter wurden die Männer der Waffen-ϟϟ, der Polizei und der Wehrmacht, die auch hier in treuer Waffenbrüderschaft unermüdlich an die Erfüllung ihrer Aufgaben herangingen und stets beispielhaft und vorbildlich ihren Mann standen. Der Einsatz ging oft vom frühen Morgen bis in die späten Nachtstunden. Nächtliche Spähtrupps, mit Lappen um die Füße gewickelt, blieben den Juden auf den Fersen und hielten sie ohne Unterbrechung unter Druck. Nicht selten wurden Juden, welche die Nacht benutzten, um aus verlassenen Bunkern ihre Lebensmittelvorräte zu ergänzen oder mit Nachbargruppen Verbindung aufzunehmen bzw. Nachrichten auszutauschen, gestellt und erledigt.

Wenn man berücksichtigt, daß die Männer der Waffen-ϟϟ zum größten Teil vor ihrem Einsatz nur eine 3- bis 4-wöchentliche Ausbildung hinter sich hatten, so muß der von ihnen gezeigte Schneid, Mut und die Einsatzfreudigkeit besonders anerkannt werden. Es ist festzustellen, daß auch die Pioniere der Wehrmacht die von ihnen vorgenommenen Sprengungen von Bunkern, Kanälen und Betonhäusern in unermüdlicher einsatzfreudiger Arbeit vollbrachten. Offiziere und Männer der Polizei, die zu einem großen Teil bereits Fronterfahrungen hatten, bewährten sich erneut durch beispielhaftes Draufgängertum.

Nur durch den ununterbrochenen und unermüdlichen Einsatz sämtlicher Kräfte ist es gelungen, insgesamt 56 065 Juden zu erfassen bzw. nachweislich zu vernichten. Dieser Zahl hinzuzusetzen sind noch die Juden, die durch Sprengungen, Brände usw. ums Leben gekommen, aber zahlenmäßig nicht erfaßt werden konnten.

Schon während der Großaktion wurde die arische Bevölkerung durch Plakatanschläge darauf hingewiesen, daß das Betreten des ehemaligen jüdischen Wohnbezirks strengstens verboten ist und daß jeder, der ohne einen gültigen Ausweis im ehemaligen jüdischen Wohnbezirk angetroffen, erschossen wird. Gleichzeitig wurde mit diesen Plakatanschlägen die arische Bevölkerung nochmals darüber belehrt,

The longer the resistance lasted, the tougher became the men of the Waffen-SS, Police, and Wehrmacht, who tirelessly fulfilled their duties in true comradeship and stood together as exemplary soldiers. Their mission often lasted from early morning to late at night. Nightly search patrols, with rags wrapped around their feet, dogged the Jews and gave them no respite. Jews who used the night to supplement their provisions from abandoned bunkers and to make contact or exchange news with neighboring groups were often brought to bay and finished off.

Considering that the greater part of the men of the Waffen-SS had been trained for only 3 or 4 weeks before this operation, they must be given special recognition for their daring, courage, and devotion to duty. It must be noted that the Wehrmacht Engineers also executed their tasks of blowing up bunkers, sewers, and concrete houses with tireless devotion. The officers and men of the Police, many already with experience at the front, again acquitted themselves with devil-may-care valor.

Only the continuous and tireless commitment of all forces made it possible to apprehend and/or destroy 56,065 Jews. To this confirmed number must be added the Jews who lost their lives in explosions, fires, etc., whose number could not be ascertained.

During the grand operation, the Aryan population was informed through posters that it was strictly forbidden to enter the former Jewish quarter and that anyone caught within the former Jewish quarter without a valid pass would be shot. Simultaneously, these posters instructed the Aryan population

daß jeder, der einem Juden wissentlich Unterschlupf gewährt, insbesondere den Juden außerhalb des jüdischen Wohnbezirks unterbringt, beköstigt oder verbirgt, mit dem Tode bestraft wird.

Der polnischen Polizei wurde genehmigt, jedem polnischen Polizisten im Falle der Festnahme eines Juden im arischen Teil der Stadt Warschau 1/3 des Barvermögens des betreffenden Juden auszuhändigen. Diese Maßnahme hat bereits Erfolge aufgewiesen.

Die polnische Bevölkerung hat die gegen die Juden durchgeführten Maßnahmen im Großen und Ganzen begrüßt. Gegen Ende der Großaktion richtete der Gouverneur einen besonderen Aufruf, der dem Unterzeichneten vor Bekanntgabe zur Genehmigung vorgelegt wurde, an die polniche Bevölkerung, mit welchem diese unter Hinweis auf die in letzter Zeit erfolgten Mordanschläge in dem Gebiet der Stadt Warschau und auf die Massengräber in Katyn über die Gründe zur Vernichtung des ehemaligen jüdischen Wohnbezirks aufgeklärt und zum Kampf gegen kommunistische Agenten und Juden aufgefordert wird (s. beiliegendes Plakat).

Die Großaktion wurde am 16.5.1943 mit der Sprengung der Warschauer Synagoge um 20,15 Uhr beendet.

Nunmehr befindet sich in dem ehemaligen jüdischen Wohnbezirk kein Betrieb mehr. Es ist alles, was an Werten, Rohstoffen und Maschinen vorhanden war, abtransportiert und verlagert worden. Alles, was an Gebäuden und sonst vorhanden war, ist vernichtet. Eine Ausnahme hiervon macht nur das sogen. Dzielna-Gefängnis der Sicherheitspolizei, welches von der Vernichtung ausgeschlossen wurde.

III

Da auch nach Durchführung der Großaktion damit zu rechnen ist, daß sich unter den Trümmern des ehemaligen jüdischen Wohnbezirks immer noch vereinzelte Juden aufhalten, muß dieses Gebiet in der näch-

once again that anyone who knowingly gave refuge to a Jew, especially if they provided shelter, food, or a hiding place to a Jew outside the Jewish quarter, would be sentenced to death.

The Polish Police was authorized to pay Polish policemen one-third of the cash belonging to any Jew they arrested within the Aryan part of Warsaw. This measure has already produced results.

The Polish population has by and large welcomed the measures implemented against the Jews. Toward the end of the grand operation, the Governor issued a special proclamation to the Polish population that was submitted to the undersigned for approval before publication. This proclamation informed them of the reasons for destroying the former Jewish quarter by referring to the recent assassinations in the city of Warsaw and the mass graves found in Katyn. They were asked to assist in the fight against Communist agents and Jews (see enclosed poster).[9]

The grand operation was terminated on 16 May 1943, with the dynamiting of the Warsaw Synagogue at 2015 hours.

Now there are no enterprises left in the former Jewish quarter. Everything of value, the raw materials, and machines have been transferred. The buildings and whatever else there was have been destroyed. The only exception is the so-called Dzielna Prison of the Security Police, which was exempted from destruction.

III

Since it must be assumed that even with the grand operation complete a few Jews are still living in the ruins of the former Jewish quarter, this area

sten Zeit gegen das arische Wohngebiet fest abgeriegelt sein und
bewacht werden. Zu diesem Zwecke ist das Polizei-Bataillon III/23
eingesetzt. Dieses Polizeibataillon hat den Auftrag, den ehemaligen jüdischen Wohnbezirk zu überwachen, insbesondere darauf zu
achten, daß niemand in das ehemalige Ghetto hineinkommt und jeden, der sich unberechtigt darin aufhält, sofort zu erschießen.
Der Kommandeur des Polizei-Bataillons erhält laufend weitere Weisungen unmittelbar vom ₰- und Polizeiführer. Es muß auf diese
Weise erreicht werden, die evtl. noch vorhandenen kleinen Über-
reste der Juden unter ständigem Druck zu halten und zu vernichten. Durch Vernichtung aller Gebäude und Schlupfwinkel und durch
Abdrosselung des Wassers muß den noch verbliebenen Juden und Banditen jede weitere Daseinsmöglichkeit genommen werden.

Es wird vorgeschlagen, das Dzielna-Gefängnis zu einem KZ. zu machen und durch die Häftlinge die Millionen von Backsteinen, den
Eisenschrott und andere Materialien auszubauen, zu sammeln und
der Verwertung zuzuführen.

Warschau, den 16. Mai 1943.

                                   Der ₰- und Polizeiführer
                                     im Distrikt Warschau

                                   ₰-Brigadeführer
                                 u.Generalmajor der Polizei.

must be guarded and firmly sealed off from the Aryan residential section for the immediate future. Police Battalion III/23 has been assigned this duty. This Police Battalion has instructions to keep watch over the former Jewish quarter, especially to prevent anyone from entering the former Ghetto and to shoot immediately any unauthorized person found there. The Commander of the Police Battalion will continue to receive further direct orders from the SS and Police Leader. In this way, it should be possible to keep the small number of Jews who might remain there under constant pressure and to destroy them. The remaining Jews and bandits must be deprived of every chance of survival through the destruction of all buildings and refuges, and the cutting of the water supply.

It is proposed to change Dzielna Prison into a concentration camp and to use the prisoners to strip down and collect the millions of bricks, scrap iron, and other materials for further utilization.

Warsaw, 16 May 1943

> SS and Police Leader in the
> Warsaw District
> (signed) Stroop
> SS Major General and Major General
> of the Police

Tägliche Meldungen.

DAILY
REPORTS

/ <u>Abschrift</u>

F e r n s c h r e i b e n

Absender: Der ϟϟ- und Polizeiführer im Distrikt Warschau

Warschau, den   2o.4.43

<u>Az.:</u> I ab -St/Gr. 16 o7 - Tgb.Nr. 516 / 43 geh.
<u>Betr.:</u> Ghettoaktion

An den
Höheren ϟϟ- und Polizeiführer Ost

<u>K r a k a u</u>

Verlauf der Aktion im Ghetto am 19.4.43:

Abschliessung des Ghettos ab 3.00 Uhr. Um 6.00 Uhr Ansetzen der
Waffen-ϟϟ in Stärke von 16/850 zur Durchkämmung des Restghettos.
Sofort nach Antreten der Einheiten starker planmässiger Feuerüberfall der Juden und Banditen. Der eingesetzte Panzer und die beiden
SPW wurden mit Molotow-Cocktails (Brandflaschen) beworfen. Panzer
brannte 2 x. Bei diesem Feuerüberfall des Gegners wurde zunächst
ein Ausweichen der eingesetzten Verbände bewirkt. Verluste beim
ersten Einsatz 12 Männer (6 ϟϟ-Männer, 6 Trawnickimänner). Etwa
8.00 Uhr zweiter Einsatz der Verbände unter Kommando des Unterzeichneten. Trotz Wiederholung eines geringeren Feuerüberfalles hatte
dieser Einsatz den Erfolg, dass die Gebäudekomplexe planmässig durchkämmt werden konnten. Es wurde erreicht, dass der Gegner sich von
den Dächern und höher gelegenen eingerichteten Stützpunkten in die
Keller bezw. Bunker und Kanäle zurückzog. Bei der Durchkämmung wurde
nur etwa 2oo Juden erfasst. Anschliessend wurden Stosstrupps auf bekannte Bunker angesetzt mit dem Auftrag, die Insassen hervorzuholen,
die Bunker zu zerstören. Judenerfassung hierdurch etwa 38o. Es
wurde der Aufenthalt der Juden in der Kanalisation festgestellt.
Die vollkommene Unterwassersetzung wurde durchgeführt, damit
Aufenthalt unmöglich. Gegen 17.30 wurde auf sehr starken Widerstand
einer Häusergruppe, auch MG.-Feuer, gestossen. Eine besondere Kampfgruppe zwang den Gegner nieder, drang in die Häuser ein, ohne den
Gegner selbst zu fassen. Die Juden und Verbrecher setzten sich von
Stützpunkt zu Stützpunkt zur Wehr, wichen im letzten Moment durch
Flucht über Dachböden oder unterirdische Gänge aus. Gegen 20.30 Uhr
wurde äussere Absperrung verstärkt. Sämtliche Einheiten aus dem
Ghetto wurden herausgezogen und in ihre Quatiere entlassen. Verstärkung der Absperrung durch 250 Männer der Waffen-ϟϟ.

Fortsetzung der Aktion am 20.4.43.
Zur Verfügung stehende Kräfte:

ϟϟ-Pz.Gren.Ers.Batl.	6/400
ϟϟ-Kav.Ersatz-Abt.	10/450
Orpo	6/165
SD	2/48
Trawnickimänner	1/150

b.w.

Copy

Teletype Message

From: SS and Police Leader in the Warsaw District

Warsaw, 20 April 1943

Ref. No.: I ab/St/Gr. 1607—*Journal No.*: 516/43 secret

Re: Ghetto operation

To:
Higher SS and Police Leader East[10]

Cracow

Progress report of the Ghetto operation on 19 April 1943:

Sealing of the Ghetto at 0300 hours. At 0600 hours, the Waffen-SS was sent into action to sweep the remnant Ghetto. Waffen-SS strength was at 16 officers and 850 men. Immediately after the units assembled, a heavy and organized surprise attack by the Jews and bandits began. The tank assigned to this operation and both heavy armored cars were pelted with Molotov cocktails (incendiary bottles). The tank was set on fire twice. During the surprise attack, our units were directed not to engage the enemy. Our losses in the first attack: 12 men (6 SS privates and 6 Trawniki men). At 0800 hours, our units went into action for the second time, under the command of the undersigned. Despite a second, less forceful attack upon us, we succeeded in our plan to sweep the blocks of buildings during this engagement. The enemy was forced to retreat from the roofs and other equipped strongholds that were located above ground level to basements or bunkers and sewers. About 200 Jews were apprehended during the sweep. Assault troops were subsequently sent against known bunkers with orders to bring out the occupants and destroy the bunkers. About 380 Jews were apprehended. The presence of Jews was detected in the sewer network. The sewers were flooded to render presence impossible. Around 1730 hours, very strong resistance, including machine-gun fire, was encountered from one group of houses. A special battle unit subdued the enemy and forced its way into the houses without apprehending the enemy. The Jews and criminals offered resistance from one stronghold after another and escaped at the last moment across attics or through subterranean passages. Around 2030 hours, the barricade surrounding the Ghetto was reinforced. All units were withdrawn from the Ghetto and dismissed to their quarters. Barricades were reinforced by 250 men of the Waffen-SS.

The operation continued on 20 April 1943.

Units at my disposal:

SS Panzer Grenadier Reserve Battalion	6 officers/400 men
SS Cavalry Reserve Division	10 officers/450 men
Order Police (Orpo)	6 officers/165 men
Security Police (SD)	2 officers/ 48 men
Trawniki men	1 officer /150 men

22

Wehrmacht

1	1o cm Haubitze	1/7
1	Flammenwerfer	1
	Pioniere	2/16
	San.Staffel	1/1
3	Flak 2.28 cm	2/24
1	franz.Panzer d.W-ϟϟ	
2	SPW d.W-ϟϟ	

zus. 31/1262

Die Führung der heutigen Aktion habe ich Herrn Major d.Sch-
S t e r n h a g e l übertragen, der von Fall zu Fall von mir
weitere Weisungen erhält.

7.oo Uhr wurden 9 Stoßtrupps in Stärke von je 1/36 aus ge-
mischten Verbänden eingesetzt, um eine intensive Durchkämmung
und Durchsuchung des Restghettos durchzuführen. Diese Durchsuch-
deren erstes Ziel um 11.oo Uhr erreicht werden soll, ist noch
Gange. Inzwischen ist festgestellt, dass in dem unbewohnten, ab
noch nicht freigegebenen Ghetto, in dem sich einige Rüstungsbetriebe und dergl. befinden, sich mehrere Widerstandsnester befinden,
die sogar verhinderten, dass der in der Nähe abgestellte Panzer
anlaufen konnte. 2 Stoßtrupps kämpften diese Widerstandsnester
nieder und bahnten den Weg für die Besatzung des Panzers. Bei diese
Unternehmen sind bereits 2 Verletzte (Waffen-ϟϟ) zu verzeichnen.

Gegner hält sich gegenüber gestern stark zurück, da ihm selbst-
verständlich die Zuteilung schwerer Waffen bekannt geworden ist.

Ich beabsichtige, Durchkämmung des Restghettos restlos durchzuführen, um anschliessend das sog. unbewohnte aber noch nicht frei-
gegebene Ghetto in gleicher Weise zu säubern. Es ist inzwischen
festgestellt, dass sich in diesem Teil des Ghettos mindestens
10 - 12 Bunker befinden, sogar in Rüstungsbetrieben. Erschwert wird
die ganze Aktion durch die sich noch im Ghetto befindenden Betriebe,
die wegen der sich in diesem befindenden Maschinen und Werkzeuge hin
sichtlich Beschuß und Brandgefahr geschützt werden müssen.

Weitere Meldung erfolgt heute abend.

Der ϟϟ- und Polizeiführer
im Distrikt Warschau

gez. Stroop

ϟϟ-Brigadeführer und
Generalmajor der Polizei.

F.d.R.d.A.:

ϟϟ-Sturmbannführer.

Wehrmacht

1 10-cm howitzer	1 officer /	7 men
1 flame thrower		1 man
Engineers	2 officers/	16 men
Medical unit	1 officer /	1 man
3 2.28-cm anti-aircraft guns	2 officers/	24 men
1 French tank of the Waffen-SS		
2 heavy armored cars of the Waffen-SS		

Total: 31 officers/1,262 men

I transferred command of today's operation to Police Major Sternhagel, subject to my further instructions as necessary.

At 0700 hours, 9 assault units drawn from mixed formations were sent into action, each with a strength of 1 officer and 36 men, to conduct an intensive sweep and search of the remnant Ghetto. The search, whose first goal shall be reached by 1100 hours, is still in progress. Meanwhile, it has been established that there are several pockets of resistance in the uninhabited part of the Ghetto, the part which is still restricted, containing several armament plants and the like. Due to the resistance, a tank that had been parked nearby could not be mobilized. Two assault units had to bear down on these pockets of resistance to clear a path for the tank crew. This operation records 2 wounded (Waffen-SS) men.

The enemy is much more cautious than he was yesterday, since he is obviously now aware that heavy weapons have been allocated.

I propose to thoroughly sweep the remnant Ghetto and then go on to purge the uninhabited but still restricted Ghetto. Meanwhile, it has been established that this part of the Ghetto, and even the armament plants themselves, contain 10 to 12 bunkers. The operation is being made more difficult by these Ghetto enterprises, whose machines and tools must be protected against bombardment and fire.

Further report will follow tonight.

> SS and Police Leader in the
> Warsaw District
>
> (signed) Stroop
>
> SS Major General and Major General
> of the Police

Certified copy
Jesuiter[11]
SS Major

Abschrift

F e r n s c h r e i b e n

Absender: Der SS- und Polizeiführer im Distrikt Warschau

Warschau, den   2o.4.43

Akz.: I ab -St/Gr- 16 07 - Tgb.Nr. 517 /43 geh.
Betr.: Ghettoaktion

An den
Höheren SS- und Polizeiführer Ost
- SS-Obergruppenführer und General der Polizei Krüger-
o.V.i.A.:

K r a k a u

Im Anschluss an das FS v.2o.4.43 - Az. Iab St/Gr 16 07, betr.
Ghettoaktion, melde ich wie folgt:

Die in dem unbewohnten noch nicht freigegebenen Ghetto festgestellten Widerstandsnester wurden durch eine Kampfgruppe der Wehrmacht
-Pionierzug und Flammenwerfer - niedergekämpft. Die Wehrmacht hatte
bei diesem Einsatz einen Verletzten durch Lungenschuß. Neun Stoßtrupps drangen bis zu der nördlichen Grenze des Ghettos vor.
9 Bunker wurden festgestellt, die sich zur Wehr setzenden Insassen
niedergekämpft, Bunker gesprengt. Die hierbei eingetretenen Verluste des Gegners sind nur unbestimmt zu ermitteln. Insgesamt wurden
durch die Tätigkeit der 9 Stoßtrupps heute 505 Juden erfasst, die,
soweit arbeitsfähig, für die Verlagerung nach Poniatowo sichergestellt wurden. Etwa gegen 15.oo Uhr setzte ich durch, dass der von
der Heeresunterkunftsverwaltung belegte Block, angeblich mit
4 ooo Juden belegt, sofort geräumt wurde. Der deutsche Verwalter
wurde aufgefordert, die jüdischen Arbeiter zum freiwilligen Verlassen aufzufordern. Diesem Ersuchen folgten nur 28 Juden. Darauf
entschloß ich mich, mit Gewalt den Häuserblock zu räumen bezw.
zu sprengen. Die hierbei eingesetzte Flak - 3 Geschütze (2 cm) -
hatte 2 Tote. Die angesetzten 10 cm Haubitze hat die Banden aus
ihren starken Befestigungen verdrängt und, soweit festgestellt
werden konnte, diesen auch Verluste beigebracht. Wegen Eintritt
der Dunkelheit mußte diese Aktion abgebrochen werden. Am 21.4.43 wird
dieses Widerstandsnest, das, soweit möglich, die Nacht über
abgeriegelt bleibt, erneut angegriffen.

Bei der heutigen Aktion wurden ausser den gemeldeten Juden erhebliche Bestände an Brandflaschen, Handgranaten, Munition, Militär-
waffenröcken und Ausrüstungsstücken erbeutet.

Verluste: 2 Tote (Wehrmacht)
            7 Verwundete (6 Waffen-SS, 1 Trawnickimann)

In einem Falle hatten die Banditen Tretminen gelegt.

Ich habe durchgesetzt, daß die Betriebe W.C. Többens, Schultz u.
Co. und Hoffmann am 21.4.43 mit der gesamten Belegschaft ab 6.00
Uhr abmarschbereit zu stehen haben, um endlich eine klare Linie
für die Bereinigung im Ghetto zu bekommen. Der Treuhänder der Többens hat sich verpflichtet, die Juden, etwa 4-5 ooo, freiwillig

./.

Copy

Teletype Message

From: SS and Police Leader in the Warsaw District

Warsaw, 20 April 1943

Ref. No.: I ab/St/Gr. 1607—*Journal No.*: 517/43 secret

Re: Ghetto operation

To:
Higher SS and Police Leader East, SS General and General of the Police
Krueger—or deputy

Cracow

Further to the teletype message of 20 April 1943, Ref. No. I ab/St/Gr. 1607,
re: Ghetto operation, I report the following:

The pockets of resistance identified in the uninhabited but still restricted
Ghetto were crushed by a battle unit of Wehrmacht Engineers and flame
throwers. In this engagement, the Wehrmacht sustained one casualty, shot
through the lungs. Nine assault parties advanced as far as the northern border
of the Ghetto. Nine bunkers were located, their resistant occupants crushed,
the bunkers blown up. Enemy losses in this engagement are indeterminable.
Activity by the 9 assault parties yielded 505 Jews; those able to work among
them were secured for transfer to Poniatowo.[12] At about 1500 hours, I succeeded in having the block of buildings that housed the Army Quartermaster's
office cleared; it supposedly quartered 4,000 Jews. The German adminis-
trator was asked to request the Jewish workers to leave the block voluntarily.
Only 28 Jews honored this request. I thereupon decided to evacuate the block
by force or to blow it up. The anti-aircraft unit assigned to this operation
(consisting of three 2-cm guns) sustained 2 deaths. The 10-cm howitzer
dislodged the gangs from their strong fortifications and, to the best of our
knowledge, inflicted losses on them. The operation had to be halted because
of darkness. On 21 April 1943, a new attack will be launched against this
pocket of resistance, which will be sealed off overnight to the greatest extent
possible.

During today's operation we captured, apart from the Jews previously reported, considerable stores of incendiary bottles, hand grenades, ammunition,
military tunics, and other equipment.

Losses: 2 dead (Wehrmacht)
    7 wounded (6 Waffen-SS men, 1 Trawniki man)

There was one instance of bandits having planted land mines.

I prevailed on the firms W. C. Toebbens,[13] Schultz & Co., and Hoffmann
to be ready for evacuation with their entire personnel on 21 April 1943 at
0600 hours so that we can at last see our way toward purging the Ghetto.
The trustee for Toebbens pledged to lead the 4,000 to 5,000 Jews on a volun-

auf den bestimmten Sammelplatz zum btransport zu führen. Gelingt wie im Falle Heeresunterkunftsverwaltung die freiwillige Herausführung nicht, werde ich mit Gewalt auch diesen Teil des Ghettos bereinigen.

Ich bestätige den mir von Obergruppenführer heute fernmündlich gegebenen Auftrag mit allen Vollmachten.

Nächste Meldung am 21.4.43, mittags.

                                    Der ᛋᛋ- und Polizeiführer
                                      im Distrikt Warschau

                                         gez. Stroop

                                    ᛋᛋ-Brigadeführer u.
                                    Generalmajor d.Polizei.

F.d.R.d.A.:

ᛋᛋ-Sturmbannführer.

tary basis to the designated assembly point for the move. If a voluntary departure proves impossible, as in the Army Quartermaster's case, I will also purge this part of the Ghetto by force.

I acknowledge receipt of the orders with full authority, communicated to me today by telephone by the General.

Next report on 21 April 1943 at noon.

SS and Police Leader in the
Warsaw District

(signed) Stroop

SS Major General and Major General
of the Police

Certified copy
Jesuiter
SS Major

<u>Abschrift</u>

F e r n s c h r e i b e n

Absender: Der ⚡⚡- und Polizeiführer im Distrikt Warschau

Warschau, den 21. 4. 43

<u>Akz.:</u> I ab -St/Gr.- 16 07 Tgb.Nr. 527/43 geh.

<u>Betr.:</u> Ghettoaktion

An den
Höheren ⚡⚡- und Polizeiführer Ost
- ⚡⚡-Obergruppenführer und General der Polizei Krüger -
o.V.i.A.

K r a k a u

Verlauf der Ghettoaktion am 21.4.43:

Im Anschluß an die heute gegen 14.00 Uhr erfolgte telefonische
Meldung berichte ich wie folgt:

Zur Verfügung stehende Kräfte wie am 20.4.43.
Beginn der Aktion: 7.00 Uhr - die Absperrung des gesamten Ghettos
                    besteht seit Beginn der Aktion am 19.4.43 unver-
                    ändert fortlaufend -

Da Teilaktion im Gebäudekomplex HUV im ostwärtigen Teil des
Ghettos am Vorabend wegen Eintritt der Dunkelheit abgebrochen
werden mußte, wurde eine Kampfgruppe, verstärkt durch Pioniere
und schwere Waffen, zur angegebenen Zeit erneut eingesetzt.
Nach Durchkämmung des riesigen Häuserblocks, bei der sich heraus-
stellte, daß eine Unmenge von Bunkern und unterirdischen Gängen
vorhanden waren, wurden etwa 60 Juden erfaßt. Trotz aller
Anstrengungen konnten von den sich in dem Block befindlichen
7 - 800 Juden mehr nicht erfasst werden. Diese zogen sich von
Schlupfwinkel zu Schlupfwinkel durch unterirdische Gänge, von
Zeit zu Zeit feuernd, immer wieder zurück. Ich entschloß mich daher,
soweit die Gänge bekannt waren, diese zu sprengen und dann den
gesamten Block in Brand zu setzen. Erst nachdem das Feuer einen
erheblichen Umfang angenommen hatte, kamen schreiende Juden zum
Vorschein, die sofort ausgesiedelt wurden. Verluste traten bei
dieser Aktion nicht ein. Es ist Vorsorge getroffen, dass das
entstandene Großfeuer lokalisiert bleibt.

Das Gros der Kräfte wurde zur Säuberung des sog. unbewohnten,
aber noch nicht freigegebenen Ghettos von Süden nach Norden
angesetzt. Vor Beginn dieser Aktion wurden aus ehem. Rüko-Betrieben
5200 Juden erfasst und unter Bedeckung nach dem zur Umlagerung
vorgesehenen Verladebahnhof verbracht. Es wurden 3 Durchsuchungs-
kommandos gebildet, die besondere Stoßtrupps zugeteilt erhielten,
um die bereits bekannten Bunker zu bekämpfen bezw. zu sprengen.
Dieses Unternehmen musste nach Durchkämmung der Hälfte des vor-
bezeichneten Raumes wegen Eintritt der Dunkelheit abgebrochen
werden.

b.w.

Copy

Teletype Message

From: SS and Police Leader in the Warsaw District

Warsaw, 21 April 1943

Ref. No.: I ab/St/Gr. 1607—*Journal No.*: 527/43 secret

Re: Ghetto operation

To:
Higher SS and Police Leader East, SS General and General of the Police
Krueger—or deputy

Cracow

Progress report of the Ghetto operation on 21 April 1943. Further to the report made by telephone today at 1400 hours, I report as follows:

Forces at my disposal were the same as on 20 April 1943.

Start of operation: 0700 hours. The blockade of the entire Ghetto which
commenced at the start of the operation on 19 April 1943, continues without
change.

Since the partial operation in the eastern part of the Ghetto in the Army
Quartermaster's building complex had to be halted yesterday due to darkness,
a battle unit reinforced by Engineers and heavy armor returned to action
at the designated time. Sweeping the huge building complex revealed a large
number of bunkers and subterranean passages. Approximately 60 Jews were
apprehended. Despite all efforts, no more of the 700 to 800 Jews located in
this block could be apprehended. They kept withdrawing through subterranean passages, moving from one hiding place to the next, firing from time
to time. I decided to blow up the passages that were known to us and then
to burn down the entire block. Only when the fire grew to considerable
proportions did screaming Jews come into view. They were immediately
removed. We had no losses in this operation. Precautions were taken to en-
sure that the resultant conflagration remains localized.

The main body of forces was committed to the cleansing of the uninhabited
but still restricted Ghetto, proceeding south to north. Before this operation
started, 5,200 Jews were apprehended who had been employed by the former
Rüko enterprises [Commission for Armament]. They were transported under
armed guard to the railroad freight yard that was designated for transshipment. Three search commandos were formed and assigned special assault
troops, with orders to attack or blow up identified bunkers. After one-half of
the designated area had been swept, the operation had to be halted due to
darkness.

Fortsetzung am 22.4.43, 7.00 Uhr.

Ausser den zu verlagernden Juden wurden 150 Juden bezw. Banditen kampfmässig erledigt, etwa 80 Banditen wurden innerhalb der Bunker durch Sprengung vernichtet. Der Gegner kämpfte heute mit den gleichen Waffen wie am Vortage, insbesondere mit selbstgefertigten Sprengkörpern. Muster sind beim ⅏- und Polizeiführer zurückbehalten. Festgestellt wurden erstmalig Angehörige der jüd.weibl.Kampforganisation (Halutzenbewegung). Erbeutet wurden: Gewehre, Pistolen, Handgranaten, Sprengkörper, Pferde und ⅏-Uniformstücke.

Eigene Verluste: 2 Orpo, 2 ⅏-Angehörige, 1 Trawnikimann (Verwundungen leichter Art).

Der ⅏- und Polizeiführer
im Distrikt Warschau

gez. Stroop

⅏-Brigadeführer u.
Generalmajor der Polizei.

F.d.R.d.A.:

⅏-Sturmbannführer.

Continued on 22 April 1943 at 0700 hours.

Besides the Jews who were to be transferred, 150 Jews or bandits were disposed of in battle. About 80 bandits were destroyed by being blown up inside their bunkers. The enemy fought today with the same weapons used yesterday, especially with homemade explosives. Samples were retained by the SS and Police Leader. For the first time we identified members of the Jewish women's fighting organization (He-halutz movement). Captured were rifles, pistols, hand grenades, explosives, horses, and parts of SS uniforms.

Our losses: 2 Order Police, 2 SS Privates, 1 Trawniki man lightly wounded

> SS and Police Leader in the
> Warsaw District
>
> (signed) Stroop
>
> SS Major General and Major General
> of the Police

Certified copy
Jesuiter
SS Major

Abschrift

F e r n s c h r e i b e n

Absender:Der ⚡⚡- und Polizeiführer im Distrikt Warschau

Warschau, den 22. April 194?

Akz.: I ab St/Gr.- 16 07 Tgb.Nr. 530/43 geh.
Betr.: Ghettoaktion - Nachtrag zu Abs. 1 v. 21.4.43.

An den
Höheren ⚡⚡- und Polizeiführer Ost
- ⚡⚡-Obergruppenführer und General der Polizei Krüger -
o.V.i.A.
K r a k a u

Die Anlegung des Brandes hatte im Laufe der Nacht das Ergebnis,
daß die unter den Dächern bezw. in den Kellern und sonstigen
Schlupfwinkeln sich trotz aller Durchsuchungsaktionen noch ver-
borgenen Juden an den äusseren Fronten des Häuserblocks zeigten,
um dem Feuer irgendwie zu entgegen. In Massen - ganze Familien -
sprangen die Juden, schon vom Feuer erfasst, aus dem Fenster oder
versuchten sich durch aneinandergeknüpfte Bettlaken usw. herabzu-
lassen. Es war Vorsorge getroffen, daß diese sowohl auch die
anderen Juden sofort liquidiert wurden. Die ganze Nacht über
wurde wiederum aus angeblich freien Gebäuden geschossen. Verluste
in der Absperrkette traten nicht ein.

Für die Verlagerung wurden 5 300 Juden erfasst und abtransportiert.

Der ⚡⚡- und Polizeiführer
im Distrikt Warschau
gez. Stroop
⚡⚡-Brigadeführer u.
Generalmajor d.Polizei

F.d.R.d.A.:

⚡⚡-Sturmbannführer.

Copy

Teletype Message

From: SS and Police Leader in the Warsaw District

Warsaw, 22 April 1943

Ref. No.: I ab/St/Gr. 1607—*Journal No.*: 530/43 secret

Re: Ghetto operation; supplement to first teletype of 21 April 1943

To:
Higher SS and Police Leader East, SS General and General of the Police
Krueger—or deputy

Cracow

During the night, the fires we had started earlier forced the Jews to appear in front of the housing blocks to escape from the flames in any way they could. Until then, they had remained hidden in attics, cellars, and other hideouts despite our search operations. Masses of burning Jews—entire families— jumped from windows or tried to lower themselves using tied-together bed sheets, etc. Measures had been taken to liquidate these as well as the other Jews immediately. Throughout the night, there was shooting once again from the buildings which had ostensibly been cleared. No losses occurred along the barricades.

5,300 Jews were apprehended for transfer and transported onward.

> SS and Police Leader in the
> Warsaw District
>
> (signed) Stroop
>
> SS Major General and Major General
> of the Police

Certified copy
Jesuiter
SS Major

A b s c h r i f t.

F e r n s c h r e i b e n

Absender: Der ⚡⚡– und Polizeiführer im Distrikt Warschau

Warschau, den 22. April 1943

Az.: I ab St/Gr 16 o7 – Tgb.Nr. 531/43 geh.
Betr.: Ghettoaktion.

An den

Höheren ⚡⚡– und Polizeiführer Ost
– ⚡⚡–Obergruppenführer und General d.Polizei Krüger –
o.V.i.A.

K r a k a u

Verlauf der Ghettoaktion am 22.4.43 bis 12 Uhr.

Mit einer Kampfgruppe wurde erneut in den nun zum größten Teil
ausgebrannten bzw. noch brennenden Häuserblock eingedrungen, um
sich noch immer dort aufhaltende Juden zu fassen. Weil aus einem
Gebäudekomplex wiederum das Feuer auf die Männer der Waffen-⚡⚡
eröffnet wurde, wurde auch hierin Feuer angelegt mit dem Erfolg,
daß nunmehr eine größere Zahl von Banditen aus ihrem Schlupfwinkel aufgescheucht und auf der Flucht erschossen wurden. Außerdem
wurden aus den Gebäudehöfen etwa 180 Juden erfaßt. Das Gros der
Einheiten nahm in Anschluß der gestern erreichten Linie die
Säuberung der nicht durchsuchten Gebäude des Ghettos vor. Diese
Aktion ist z.Zt. noch im Gange. Wie in den Vortagen wurde ört-
licher Widerstand gebrochen und die aufgefundenen Bunker gesprengt. Leider ist nicht zu verhindern, daß ein Teil der Banditen und Juden sich in den Kanälen unterhalb des Ghettos aufhält
und kaum zu fassen ist, weil die Unterwassersetzung von diesen
unterbrochen wurde. Die Stadtverwaltung ist nicht in der Lage,
diesen Übelstand zu beheben. Das Anbringen von Nebelkerzen und
die Vermengung des Wassers mit Chreosot hatte ebenfalls nicht
den gewünschten Erfolg. Verbindung mit der Wehrmacht tadellos.

Der ⚡⚡– und Polizeiführer
im Distrikt Warschau

gez. Stroop

⚡⚡–Brigadeführer und
Generalmajor der Polizei.

F.d.R.d.A.

[signature]

⚡⚡–Sturmbannführer.

Copy

Teletype Message

From: SS and Police Leader in the Warsaw District

Warsaw, 22 April 1943

Ref. No.: I ab/St/Gr. 1607—*Journal No.*: 531/43 secret

Re: Ghetto operation

To:

Higher SS and Police Leader East, SS General and General of the Police
Krueger—or deputy

Cracow

Progress report of the Ghetto operation on 22 April 1943 up to 1200 hours.

One battle unit was again dispatched to invade the largely burned-out or
still burning housing blocks in order to apprehend remaining Jews. Because
the men of the Waffen-SS were again fired upon from one block of buildings,
this block, too, was set on fire. The result was that a considerable number of
bandits were frightened out of their hiding places and shot while trying to
escape. We apprehended an additional 180 Jews in the courtyards of buildings. The main body of our forces proceeded with the cleansing of the un-
searched Ghetto buildings, starting from the line where the operation had
ended yesterday. This operation is still in progress. Local resistance, as on
previous days, was broken and the bunkers that were discovered blown up.
Unfortunately, it is impossible to prevent some Jews and bandits from taking
refuge in the sewers below the Ghetto, where they are difficult to apprehend,
since they disrupted the flooding operation. The city administration is not
in a position to remedy this inconvenience. Neither the use of smoke candles
nor mixing creosote into the water had the desired results. Liaison with the
Wehrmacht has been excellent.

SS and Police Leader in the
Warsaw District

(signed) Stroop

SS Major General and Major General
of the Police

Certified copy
Jesuiter
SS Major

A b s c h r i f t .

F e r n s c h r e i b e n

Absender: Der ⚡-und Polizeiführer im Distrikt Warschau

Warschau, den 22. 4. 1943

Az.: I ab -St/Gr.- 16 o7 -Tgb.Nr. 532/43 geh.
Betr.: Ghettoaktion.

An den
Höheren ⚡- und Polizeiführer Ost
- ⚡-Obergruppenführer und General d.Polizei Krüger -
o.V.i.A.
K r a k a u

Verlauf der Ghettoaktion am 22.4.43. Meldung über die Aktion
bis 12.00 Uhr ist bereits durch FS von heute erstattet.

Anschließend wird folgendes gemeldet:

Die schon erwähnte Durchsuchung der restlichen Gebäudekomplexe
durch angesetzte Stoßtrupps, die teilweise Widerstand antrafen,
hatte folgenden Erfolg: 1loo Juden zur Verlagerung erfaßt, 2o3
Banditen und Juden erschossen, 15 Bunker gesprengt. Es wurden
erbeutet: 8o Brandflaschen und andere Beute.

Zur Verfügung stehende Kräfte: Wie durch FS v. 2o.4.43 Tgb.Nr.
516/43 geh., gemeldet.

Eigene Verluste: ⚡-Untersturmführer Dehmke (Tot) feindl. Schuß in
⚡-Kav.Ers.Abt. eine von ihm getragene Hand-
granate
1 Wm.d.Polizei (Lungendurchschuß).

Bei Sprengungen der Bunker durch die Pioniere sind eine erhebliche Zahl von Juden und Banditen unter den Trümmern begraben.
Es war in einer Reihe von Fällen notwendig, zur Ausräucherung
der Banden Brände anzulegen.

Es ist noch zu melden, daß immer wieder Teile der eingesetzten
Verbände seit gestern auch von außerhalb des Chettos, also aus
dem arischen Teil, beschossen werden. Sofort eindringenden Stoßtrupps gelang es, in einem Falle 35 poln. Banditen, Kommunisten
zu fassen, die sofort liquidiert wurden. Bei heute notwendigen
Erschießungen ist es wiederholt vorgekommen, daß die Banditen
mit dem Ruf "Hoch lebe Polen", "Es lebe Moskau" zusammenbrachen.

Die Aktion wird am 23.4.43, 7.oo Uhr, fortgesetzt.

Der ⚡- und Polizeiführer
im Distrikt Warschau

gez. Stroop
⚡-Brigadeführer u.
Generalmajor der Polizei.

F.d.R.d.A.

⚡-Sturmbannführer.

Copy

Teletype Message

From: SS and Police Leader in the Warsaw District

Warsaw, 22 April 1943

Ref. No.: I ab/St/Gr. 1607—*Journal No.*: 532/43 secret

Re: Ghetto operation

To:
Higher SS and Police Leader East, SS General and General of the Police
Krueger—or deputy

Cracow

Progress report of the Ghetto operation on 22 April 1943. Report on operation until 1200 hours already submitted today by earlier teletype message. I continue with the following report:

The already mentioned search by assault units of the remaining blocks of buildings met partial resistance. It had the following results: 1,100 Jews apprehended for transfer, 203 Jews and bandits shot, 15 bunkers blown up. 80 incendiary bottles and other booty were captured.

Units at my disposal: same as reported by teletype message on 20 April 1943, Journal No. 516/43 secret.

Our losses: SS Second Lieutenant Dehmke of the SS-Cavalry Reserve Division dead; enemy hit a hand grenade he was carrying. 1 Sergeant of the Police shot through the lung.

When the Engineers blew up the bunkers, considerable numbers of Jews and bandits were buried under the ruins. On a number of occasions, fires had to be set to smoke out the gangs.

It must be further reported that since yesterday, some of our formations have been repeatedly shot at from outside the Ghetto—*i.e.*, from the Aryan part. Assault units immediately entered the area in question and in one case succeeded in apprehending 35 Polish bandits, Communists, who were liquidated at once. At executions, which became necessary today, bandits repeatedly collapsed shouting "Long live Poland!" and "Long live Moscow!"

The operation will be continued on 23 April 1943 at 0700 hours.

SS and Police Leader in the
Warsaw District

(signed) Stroop

SS Major General and Major General
of the Police

Certified copy
Jesuiter
SS Major

<u>A b s c h r i f t</u>

F e r n s c h r e i b e n

Absender: Der ⚡⚡– und Polizeiführer im Distrikt Warschau

                                 Warschau, den   23.4.1943

<u>Az.:</u> I ab -St/Gr- 16 o7 - Tgb.Nr. 538/43 geh.
<u>Betr.:</u> Ghettoaktion

An den

Höheren ⚡⚡– und Polizeiführer Ost
- ⚡⚡–Obergruppenführer und General d.Polizei Krüger -
o.V.i.A.

K r a k a u

Verlauf der Ghettoaktion am 23.4.43

Beginn: 7.oo Uhr.

Das gesamte ehemalige Ghetto war zur heutigen Durchkämmung in
24 Bezirke eingeteilt. In jedem Bezirk wurde 1 verstärkter
Durchsuchungsstoßtrupp mit besonderem Auftrag entsandt. Für die
den Durchsuchungsstoßtrupps gegebenen Aufträge hatten diese Zeit
bis 16.oo Uhr.

Erfolg dieses Unternehmens: 600 Juden und Banditen aufgestöbert
und erfaßt und etwa 2oo Juden und Banditen erschossen. 48 Bunker,
teilweise raffiniertester Art, wurden gesprengt. Erbeutet wurden
– Wertgegenständen, Geld – auch einige Gasmasken.

Es war den Einheiten bekanntgegeben, daß die Aktion mit dem heutigen Tage beendet werden sollte. Diese Mitteilung war bereits
vormittags bei den Juden bekannt. Aus diesem Grunde wurden nach
etwa 1 – 1 1/2-stündiger Pause Durchsuchungsstoßtrupps erneut
angesetzt mit dem Erfolg, wie es stets der Fall ist, die Anwesenheit von Juden und Banditen in verschiedenen Blocks festgestellt wurde. Aus einem Gebäudekomplex wurden die Absperrmann-
schaften sogar beschossen. Eine besondere Kampfgruppe wurde hier-
gegen angesetzt und zur Ausräucherung der Banditen sämtliche Gebäude in Brand gesetzt. Die Juden und Banditen hielten sich bis
zum letzten Augenblick, um dann die Männer der Einheiten mit
Feuer zu belegen. Sogar mit Karabinern wurde geschossen. Eine
Anzahl von Balkonen schießende Banditen wurde durch Schüsse zum
Absturz gebracht.

Am heutigen Tage ist auch die angebliche Zentrale der "PPR" un-
besetzt festgestellt und vernichtet worden. An diesem 5. Tage
wurden sichtbar die größten Terroristen und Aktivisten gestellt,
die es verstanden haben, sich jeder bisher stattgefundenen Über-
holung bzw. Verlagerung zu entziehen.

                                          b.w.

Copy

Teletype Message

From: SS and Police Leader in the Warsaw District

Warsaw, 23 April 1943

Ref. No.: I ab/St/Gr. 1607—*Journal No.*: 538/43 secret

Re: Ghetto operation

To:
Higher SS and Police Leader East, SS General and General of the Police
Krueger—or deputy

Cracow

Progress report of the Ghetto operation on 23 April 1943. Start of operation: 0700 hours.

The entire former Ghetto was divided into 24 districts for today's sweep. One reinforced assault search party was dispatched to each district with special orders. The assault search parties were given until 1600 hours to carry out these orders.

Results of this operation: 600 Jews and bandits routed out and apprehended, and about 200 Jews and bandits shot. 48 bunkers, some of them most artful, were demolished. Besides money and valuables, several gas masks were captured.

Notice had been given to all units that the operation would be terminated today. By this morning, this information was already known to the Jews. For this reason, assault search parties were again dispatched after a pause of 1 to 1½ hours. The result, as usual, was that we established the presence of Jews and bandits in various blocks. The blockade detail was even shot at from one building complex. A special battle unit was dispatched, and all the buildings were set on fire to smoke out the bandits. The Jews and bandits stood fast until the last moment and then concentrated their gunfire on our units. Even carbines were fired. A number of bandits firing from balconies were hit and came crashing down.

Today also, the so-called headquarters of the PPR[14] was discovered unoccupied and destroyed. On this fifth day of operations, the leading terrorists and activists have been taken, those who had managed to evade every takeover or transfer until now.

Nach Meldung eines Volksdeutschen sind wiederum Juden durch die Kanalisation in den arischen Stadtteil geflohen. Es wurde verraten, daß sich in einem Hause einige Juden aufhielten. Ein besonders motorisiert angesetzter Stoßtrupp drang in das Gebäude ein und konnte 3 Juden, darunter 2 Jüdinnen, noch festnehmen. Während dieser Aktion wurde der Lkw. mit einer Brandflasche und einem Sprengkörper beworfen, wodurch 2 Männer der Orpo durch Verwundung ausfielen.

Die ganze Aktion wird erschwert durch die mit allen Raffinessen vorgehenden Juden und Banditen, z.B. wurde festgestellt, daß in den Leichenwagen, mit denen die herumliegenden Toten gesammelt werden, gleichzeitig lebende Juden auf den jüdischen Friedhof gefahren werden und damit außerhalb des Ghettos entkommen. Durch ständige Kontrolle der Leichenwagen wird auch dieser Weg zur Flucht unterbunden.

Bei Abbruch der heutigen Unternehmung gegen 22.00 Uhr wurde festgestellt, daß wiederum etwa 3o Banditen in einen sog. Rüstungsbetrieb wechselten, um dort Unterschlupf zu finden. Da in diesem Betrieb große Werte der Wehrmacht lagern, ist dieser aufgefordert, bis 24.4. mittags zu räumen, um dieses Häuserlabyrinth ebenfalls morgen in Angriff zu nehmen.

Zur Verlagerung aus den Betrieben wurden heute 3 5oo Juden erfaßt. Insgesamt wurden bis heute zur Verlagerung erfaßt bzw. bereits abtransportiert: 19 45o Juden. Von diesen Juden sind z.Zt. noch etwa 2 5oo zu verladen. der nächste Zug fährt am 24.4.43 ab.

Kräfte wie am 22.4.43 – ohne 15o Trawnikimänner –. Diese sind bereits dem KdO. zur Verstärkung für eine andere Aufgabe zugeteilt.

Eigene Verluste: 2 Pol.Wm. (SB) verwundet
                  1 Trawnikimann verwundet.

Fortsetzung der Aktion am 24.4.43, 1o.oo Uhr. Dieser Zeitpunkt wurde gewählt, um die sich etwa noch im Ghetto befindenen Juden in dem Glauben zu lassen, daß die Aktion heute tatsächlich beendet wurde.

                          Der SS- und Polizeiführer
                            im Distrikt Warschau

                                gez. Stroop
                              SS-Brigadeführer u.
                              Generalmajor der Polizei.

F.d.R.d.A.

SS-Sturmbannführer.

An ethnic German[15] reported that once again Jews had escaped through the sewers to the Aryan part of the city. Informers reported that several Jews were hiding in a house. A special motorized assault search party invading the building was able to capture 3 Jews, including 2 Jewesses. During this operation, our truck was pelted with an incendiary bottle and an explosive; 2 members of the Order Police were wounded and put out of action.

The operation is being made more difficult by the cunning ways in which the Jews and bandits behave. For example, we discovered that the wagons used to collect the scattered corpses were also carting live Jews to the Jewish cemetery, thus enabling them to escape outside the Ghetto. The continuous search of these wagons will close off this escape route.

At the conclusion of today's operations, around 2200 hours, it was discovered that once again 30 bandits had moved over to a so-called armament enterprise to find refuge. Because the Wehrmacht stores goods of great value in this plant, the request was made to clear it by noon on 24 April, so that this labyrinth of houses can be attacked tomorrow.

Today 3,500 Jews were apprehended for transfer from the enterprises. Until today, a total of 19,450 Jews was apprehended for transfer or already transported onward; 2,500 of these Jews are still to be loaded. The next train departs on 24 April 1943.

Our strength: the same as on 22 April 1943, less 150 Trawniki men. These have been reassigned to the Commander of the Order Police as reinforcements for another mission.

Our losses: 2 Polish Police (SB[16]) wounded, 1 Trawniki man wounded

Operations to be continued on 24 April 1943 at 1000 hours. This time was chosen to make the Jews who are remaining in the Ghetto believe that the operation had definitely ended today.

SS and Police Leader in the
Warsaw District

(signed) Stroop

SS Major General and Major General
of the Police

Certified copy
Jesuiter
SS Major

A b s c h r i f t .

F e r n s c h r e i b e n

Absender: Der ⁄⁄- und Polizeiführer im Distrikt Warschau

                                        Warschau, den   24. 4. 43

Akz.: I ab - St/Wdt. - 16 o7 Tgb.Nr. 545/43 geh.

Betr.: Ghettoaktion.

An den

Höheren ⁄⁄- und Polizeiführer Ost
- ⁄⁄-Obergruppenführer und General der Polizei Krüger -
o.V.i.A.

K r a k a u

Verlauf der Aktion am 24.4.43, Beginn: 1o.oo Uhr.

Zum Unterschied von den Vortagen wurden die heute wiederum
gebildeten 24 Durchsuchungsstoßtrupps nicht von einer Seite
sondern gleichzeitig von allen Enden des Ghettos zur Durchkämmung
angesetzt. Scheinbar sind die noch vorhandenen Juden dadurch,
daß das Unternehmen erst um 1o.oo Uhr begann, in dem Glauben gewesen, die Angelegenheit wäre am Vortage beendet gewesen. Der
Erfolg der Durchsuchungsaktion war deswegen am heutigen Tage
besonders erfolgreich. Der Erfolg beruht aber auch auf der Tatsache, daß die Unterführer und Männer sich inzwischen an dem
hinterhältigen Kampf und an die Schliche der Juden und Banditen
gewöhnt haben, vor allem große Geschicklichkeit in der Aufspürung
von den unzähligen vorhandenen Bunkern bekommen haben. Nach
Rückkehr der Stoßtrupps wurde heute gegen Abend ein besonderer
Häuserblock im nordöstlichen Teil des ehemaligen Ghettos ange-
packt. In diesem Häuserlabyrinth befand sich eine sogenannte
Rüstungsfirma die angeblich Millionenwerte in Wehrmachtsgut zum
Verarbeiten und Lagern haben sollte. Ich hatte der Wehrmacht am
23.4.43 gegen 21.oo Uhr Kenntnis von meiner Absicht gegeben mit
dem Ersuchen, das Wehrmachtsgut bis 12.00 Uhr abzufahren. Da die
Wehrmacht erst gegen 1o.oo Uhr mit der Abfahrt begann, mußte ich
eine Verlängerung bis 18.oo Uhr einräumen. Um 18.15 Uhr trat die
Durchsuchungskampfgruppe nach Abriegelung in die Gebäude ein und
stellte die Anwesenheit einer großen Anzahl von Juden fest. Da
diese Juden zum Teil Widerstand leisteten gab ich den Befehl zum
ausbrennen. Erst nachdem der Straßenzug und zu beiden Seiten
sämtliche Höfe in hellen Flammen standen, kamen die Juden zum
Teil brennend aus den Häuserblocks hervor bzw. versuchten sich
durch einen Sprung aus den Fenstern und Balkonen auf die Straße,
auf die sie vorher Betten, Decken und sonstige Teile geworfen
hatten, zu retten. Immer wieder konnte man beobachten, daß trotz
der großen Feuersnot Juden und Banditen es vorzogen, lieber wieder ins Feuer zurückzugehen, als in unsere Hände zu fallen.Immer
wieder schossen die Juden bis fast zur Beendigung der Aktion,
sodaß noch fast am Ende dieses Tages die Pioniergruppe unter
LMG-Schutz in ein besonders starkes Betonhaus eindringen mußte.

Ende der heutigen Aktion: Am 25.4.43 um 1.45 Uhr.

Es wurden zur Verlagerung 166o Juden eingebracht. Aus Bunkern
wurden hervorgezogen 1814, erschossen ca. 33o. Ungezählte Juden

                                                        b.w.

Teletype Message

From: SS and Police Leader in the Warsaw District

Warsaw, 24 April 1943

Ref. No.: I ab/St/Wdt. 1607—*Journal No.*: 545/43 secret

Re: Ghetto operation

To:

Higher SS and Police Leader East, SS General and General of the Police Krueger—or deputy

Cracow

Progress report of the Ghetto operation on 24 April 1943. Start of operation: 1000 hours.

In contrast to previous days, the 24 assault search parties, which were again dispatched today, did not start their sweep of the Ghetto from one flank only but proceeded simultaneously from all sides. Since the operation did not start until 1000 hours, the remaining Jews apparently believed that the matter had ended yesterday. Today's search operation was therefore especially successful. But our success is also due to the fact that the noncommissioned officers and men have become accustomed to the underhanded fighting and tricks of the Jews and bandits, and have acquired great skill in tracking down the innumerable bunkers. Today, toward evening, after the return of the assault parties, a particular block of houses in the northeastern part of the former Ghetto was taken on. This labyrinth of buildings housed a so-called armament firm where military goods supposedly worth millions were manufactured and stored. On 23 April 1943, about 2100 hours, I notified the Wehrmacht of my intention and requested that they remove their goods by 1200 hours. Since the Wehrmacht did not start to move until 1000 hours, I had to extend the time limit to 1800 hours. At 1815 hours, the buildings were sealed off. An assault search party forced its entry and discovered that a large number of Jews were present. Since some of the Jews resisted, I ordered the buildings burned down. Only after the street and courtyards were ablaze did the Jews come out of the housing blocks. Many were on fire, and they tried to save themselves by jumping from windows or balconies into the street below, where they had previously flung beds, blankets, and other articles. Again and again, one could observe that the Jews and bandits, notwithstanding the gigantic conflagration, preferred to go back into the fire rather than fall into our hands. The Jews continued to shoot almost until the end of the operation. Toward the end of the day, a unit of engineers had to make their way under machine-gun protection into a specially reinforced concrete building.

End of today's operation: 25 April 1943 at 0145 hours.

Today, 1,660 Jews were collected for transfer; 1,814 were pulled out of bunkers, circa 330 shot. Countless Jews burned to death or perished in

verbrannten oder kamen in den gesprengten Bunkern um. Es wurden 26
Bunker gesprengt und eine nicht gezählte Menge an Geldscheinen,
hierunter besonders Dollars, eingebracht.

Eigene Kräfte: Wie am Vortage, weniger 50 Mann Waffen-SS.

Eigene Verluste: 2 SS-Männer und ein Trawniki-Mann verwundet.

Insgesamt wurden bisher 25.500 Juden, die im ehem. jüd. Wohnbezirk
gewohnt haben, durch die laufende Aktion erfaßt. Da über den Bestand
an Juden nur unklare Schätzungen vorliegen, nehme ich an, daß sich
im Ghetto nur noch ganz geringe Teile der Juden und Banditen aufhalten.

Fortsetzung der Aktion am 25.4.43 um 13.00 Uhr.

Ich bestätige den Empfang der FS. Nr. 1222 und 1223 vom 24.4.43.
Soweit zu übersehen, wird die laufende große Aktion bis einschließlich 2. Ostertag andauern.

An den Außenmauern des Ghettos sind bereits heute Plakate angebracht
die bekannt geben, daß jeder, der das ehem. Ghetto betritt ohne sich
legitimieren zu können, erschossen wird.

Der SS- und Polizeiführer
in Distrikt Warschau

gez. Stroop
SS-Brigadeführer u.
Generalmajor d.Polizei.

F.d.R.d.A.

[signature]

SS-Sturmbannführer.

blown-up bunkers. 26 bunkers were blown up and an uncounted quantity of paper money, especially dollars, gathered.

Our forces: same as on the preceding day, minus 50 Waffen-SS men

Our losses: 2 SS Privates and 1 Trawniki man wounded

Altogether, a total of 25,500 Jews who lived in the former Jewish quarter have been apprehended in the current operation. Since there are only vague estimates as to the strength of the Jews, I assume that only very small numbers of Jews and bandits still remain within the Ghetto.

Operation to be continued on 25 April 1943 at 1300 hours.

I confirm receipt of teletype messages Nos. 1222 and 1223 of 24 April 1943. As far as can be foreseen, the current grand operation will last until the second day of Easter [26 April 1943].

Posters were affixed on the outside walls of the Ghetto today announcing that anyone entering the former Ghetto without valid papers will be shot.

> SS and Police Leader in the
> Warsaw District
>
> (signed) Stroop
>
> SS Major General and Major General
> of the Police

Certified copy
Jesuiter
SS Major

<u>Abschrift</u>

F e r n s c h r e i b e n

Absender: Der ℋ– und Polizeiführer im Distrikt Warschau

Warschau, den 25.4.43

<u>Akz.:</u> I ab-St/Wdt.-1607 Tgb.Nr.549/43 geh.

<u>Betr.:</u> Ghettoaktion.

An den

Höheren ℋ– und Polizeiführer Ost
– ℋ–Obergruppenführer und General der Polizei Krüger –
o.V.i.A.

K r a k a u

Verlauf der Aktion am 25.4.43, Beginn 13.00 Uhr.

Es wurden für den heutigen Tag 7 Durchkämmungsstoßtrupps gebildet, Stärke 1/70, denen je ein bestimmter Häuserblock zugewiesen wurde.

Auftrag:" Nochmalige Durchkämmung sämtlicher Gebäude, Feststellung von Bunkern und Sprengung derselben, sowie Erfassung der Juden. Dort wo sie irgendwie Widerstand leisten oder die Bunker nicht erreicht werden können, sind die Gebäude niederzubrennen."

Neben der Tätigkeit dieser 7 Durchkämmungsstoßtrupps wurde ein besonderes Unternehmen gegen ein ausserhalb der ehem. Ghettomauer liegendes Banditennest unternommen, welches nur von Polen bewohnt war.

Das heutige Unternehmen endete bei fast sämtlichen Stoßtrupps damit, dass Riesenbrände entstanden und dadurch die Juden zum Verlassen ihrer Verstecke und Schlupfwinkel veranlaßte. Es wurden insgesamt 1690 Juden lebend erfasst. Nach Erzählung der Juden sind hierunter mit Bestimmtheit abgesetzte Fallschirmspringer und solche Banditen, die von einer unbekannten Stelle mit Waffen beliefert wurden. 274 Juden wurden erschossen und wie an allen Tagen ungezählte Juden in gesprengten Bunkern verschüttet und wie immer wieder festgestellt werden kann, verbrannt. Mit der heutigen Beute an Juden sind meines Erachtens ein sehr grosser Teil der Banditen und niedrigsten Elemente des Ghettos erfasst worden. Die sofortige Liquidierung wurde wegen Eintritt der Dunkelheit nicht mehr durchgeführt. Ich werde versuchen, für morgen einen Zug nach T II zu erhalten, andernfalls die Liquidierung morgen durchgeführt wird. Auch am heutigen Tage wurde wiederholt Widerstand mit Waffen geleistet und in einem Bunker 3 Pistolen und Sprenkörper erbeutet. Ferner wurden am heutigen Tage erhebliche Bestände an Papiergeld, Devisen, Goldmünzen und Schmuckgegenständen sichergestellt. Die Juden verfügen immer noch über erhebliche Vermögenswerte. Wenn gestern nacht das ehem. Ghetto von einem Feuerschein überzogen war, so ist heute abend ein riesiges Feuermeer zu sehen. Da bei den planmässigen und regelmässigen Durchkämmungen immer wieder Juden in grosser Zahl aufgespürt werden, wird die Aktion am 26.4.43 fortgesetzt. Beginn 10.00 Uhr.

b.w.

Copy

Teletype Message

From: SS and Police Leader in the Warsaw District

Warsaw, 25 April 1943

Ref. No.: I ab/St/Wdt. 1607—*Journal No.*: 549/43 secret

Re: Ghetto operation

To:
Higher SS and Police Leader East, SS General and General of the Police Krueger—or deputy

Cracow

Progress report of the Ghetto operation on 25 April 1943. Start of operation: 1300 hours.

Today, 7 assault sweep detachments were formed. Strength: 1 officer and 70 men; each was assigned to a specific block of houses.

Order: "Renewed sweep of all buildings; discovery of bunkers and their demolition; apprehension of any Jews. Wherever they offer resistance or bunkers are beyond reach, the buildings are to be burned down."

In addition to the activity of these 7 assault sweep detachments, a special operation was mounted against a covey of bandits located outside the former Ghetto walls, which was housing Poles only.

Today's operation ended for almost all assault units with gigantic fires, which induced the Jews to leave their hiding places and refuges. A total of 1,690 Jews was apprehended alive. According to Jewish accounts, these definitely included parachutists who had been dropped and bandits who had been supplied with weapons from an unknown source. A total of 274 Jews was shot. As on previous days, uncounted Jews were buried under the rubble of demolished bunkers and burned to death, as we discover all the time. In my opinion, today's booty of Jews encompassed a very large part of the bandits and the lowest elements of the Ghetto. Because darkness set in, we did not proceed with immediate liquidation. I will try to obtain a train for T II [Treblinka] tomorrow.[17] Otherwise, the liquidation will be carried out tomorrow. There was armed resistance again today. In one bunker, 3 pistols and explosives were captured. Further, considerable amounts of paper money, foreign currency, gold coins, and jewelry were secured today. The Jews still have considerable wealth at their disposal. During last night, a glare of fires hovered over the former Ghetto; this evening one can see a gigantic sea of flames. Since large numbers of Jews continue to be discovered during each systematic and regular sweep, the operation will be continued on 26 April 1943, starting at 1000 hours.

Mit dem heutigen Tage wurden insgesamt 27.464 Juden des ehem.jüd.
Ghettos Warschau erfasst.

Eigene Kräfte: Wie am Vortage.

Eigene Verluste: 3 Angehörige der Waffen-SS und ein Angehöriger der
Sicherheitspolizei verwundet.

Bisherige Gesamtverluste:

Waffen-SS	27	Verwundete
Ordnungspolizei	9	"
Sicherheitspolizei	4	"
Wehrmacht	1	"
Trawniki-Männer	9	"
	50	Verwundete

und 5 Tote, davon:

Waffen-SS	2	Tote
Wehrmacht	2	"
Trawniki-Männer	1	"
	5	Tote

Der SS- und Polizeiführer
im Distrikt Warschau

gez: Stroop

SS-Brigadeführer u.
Generalmajor d.Polizei

F.d.R.d.A-:

SS-Sturmbannführer.

As of today, a total of 27,464 Jews of the former Warsaw Jewish Ghetto has been apprehended.

Our forces: same as on the previous day

Our losses: 3 members of the Waffen-SS and 1 member of the Security Police wounded

Total losses to this date:

Waffen-SS	27 wounded
Order Police	9 wounded
Security Police	4 wounded
Wehrmacht	1 wounded
Trawniki men	9 wounded
	50 wounded

and 5 dead, consisting of:

Waffen-SS	2 dead
Wehrmacht	2 dead
Trawniki men	1 dead
	5 dead

SS and Police Leader in the
Warsaw District

(signed) Stroop

SS Major General and Major General
of the Police

Certified copy
Jesuiter
SS Major

A b s c h r i f t !
F e r n s c h r e i b e n

Absender: Der ⚡⚡- und Polizeiführer im Distrikt Warschau

Warschau, den 26.4.43

<u>Az.:</u>   I ab St/Wdt - 16 07 - Tgb.Nr. 550/43 geh.
<u>Betr.:</u>   Ghetto-Großaktion - Ergänzungsmeldung

An den

Höheren ⚡⚡- und Polizeiführer Ost
⚡⚡-Obergruppenführer und General der Polizei Krüger
o.V.i.A.

<u>K r a k a u</u>

1.) Die Aktion am 25.4.43 wurde um 22.oo Uhr beendet.

2.) Allgemeine Auswirkungen der Durchführung der Aktion:

Die in Warschau lebenden Polen sind stark beeindruckt über die
Härte des Zupackens im ehem. jüd. Wohnbezirk. Wie aus den Er-
eignismeldungen zu ersehen, ist seit der laufenden Aktion eine
allgemeine Beruhigung, abgesehen von kleineren Vorfällen, ein-
getreten, insbesondere im Stadtgebiet Warschau. Daraus ist zu
folgern, daß die Banditen und Saboteure bisher im ehem. jüd.
Wohnbezirk lebten und nunmehr vernichtet wurden.

Hierbei interessiert die Tatsache, daß bei einem Brand eines Gebäudes, in dem z.Zt. bearbeiteten Wohnbezirk, ein illegales Munitionslager in die Luft ging.

Für die Richtigkeit: Der ⚡⚡- und Polizeiführer
                                        im Distrikt Warschau

[Unterschrift]   gez. Stroop

⚡⚡-Sturmbannführer.   ⚡⚡-Brigadeführer
                                   u. Generalmajor d. Polizei

Copy

Teletype Message

From: SS and Police Leader in the Warsaw District

Warsaw, 26 April 1943

Ref. No.: I ab/St/Wdt. 1607—*Journal No.*: 550/43 secret

Re: Grand operation in the Ghetto; supplemental report

To:
Higher SS and Police Leader East, SS General and General of the Police
Krueger—or deputy

Cracow

1.) The operation on 25 April 1943 was ended at 2200 hours.

2.) General consequences of its implementation: The Poles living in Warsaw are deeply impressed by the toughness of our intervention in the former Jewish quarter. It is evident from the reported course of events that a general pacification, notwithstanding small incidents, has occurred since the beginning of the current operation, especially within the city of Warsaw. We draw the conclusion that the bandits and saboteurs had been living in the former Jewish quarter and have been destroyed.

In this connection, it will be of interest that an illegal ammunition cache exploded in a burning building in the very district in which we are doing work.

> SS and Police Leader in the
> Warsaw District
>
> (signed) Stroop
>
> SS Major General and Major General
> of the Police

Certified copy
Jesuiter
SS Major

A b s c h r i f t !
F e r n s c h r e i b e n

Absender: Der ∦- und Polizeiführer im Distrikt Warschau

Warschau, den 26.4.43

Az.: I ab St/Wdt. - 16 07 - Tgb.Nr. 551/43 geh.
Betr.: Ghettoaktion

An den

Höheren ∦- und Polizeiführer Ost
∦-Obergruppenführer und General der Polizei Krüger
o.V.i.A.

K r a k a u

Beginn der Aktion 10.oo Uhr.

Der gesamte ehem. jüd. Wohnbezirk wurde heute wiederum durch
dieselben Durchsuchungsstoßtrupps mit denselben Bezirken durchkämmt. Hierbei wollte ich erreichen, daß die Führer in die ihnen
nunmehr bekannten Straßenzüge bzw. Häuserblocks und Höfe gelan-
gen, um immer weiter in das Wirrwarr von Bunkern und unterirdischen Gängen eindringen zu können. Fast ohne Ausnahme meldeten
die Stoßtrupps Widerstände, die aber durch Erwiderung des Feuers
oder durch Sprengung der Bunker restlos gebrochen wurden. Es
zeigt sich immer mehr, daß nunmehr die Reihe an die zähesten
und widerstandsfähigsten Juden und Banditen kommt. Es sind mehrfach Bunker gewaltsam geöffnet worden, deren Insassen seit der
Dauer der Aktion nicht mehr an die Oberfläche gekommen waren.
In einer Reihe von Fällen waren die Insassen der Bunker nach
der erfolgten Sprengung kaum noch in der Lage, an die Oberfläche
zu kriechen. Nach Aussagen der gefangenen Juden sollen in den/
Bunkern eine größere Anzahl der Insassen von der Hitze und
dem Qualm und von den erfolgten Sprengungen irre geworden sein.

Es wurden verschiedene Juden festgenommen, die mit der polnischen Terroristengruppe enge Verbindung hielten und zusammen
gearbeitet hatten. Außerhalb des ehem. jüd. Wohnbezirks wurden
29 Juden festgenommen.

Im Verlaufe der heutigen Aktion wurden mehrere Häuserblocks
niedergebrannt. Dieses ist die einzige und letzte Methode, um
dieses Gesindel und Untermenschentum an die Oberfläche zu zwingen.

Es wurden wiederum Waffen-Brandflaschen, Sprengkörper und größere Mengen Geld und Devisen erbeutet.

Auch heute habe ich veranlaßt, daß mehrere sogen. Rüstungs- und
wehrwirtschaftliche Betriebe unverzüglich ihre noch vorhandenen
Bestände verlagern, damit auch diese Häuserblocks, in die nunmehr
die Juden unter dem Schutze der Bewaffnung der deutschen Wehr-

Copy

Teletype Message

From: SS and Police Leader in the Warsaw District

Warsaw, 26 April 1943

Ref. No.: I ab/St/Wdt. 1607—*Journal No.*: 551/43 secret

Re: Ghetto operation

To:
Higher SS and Police Leader East, SS General and General of the Police
Krueger—or deputy

Cracow

Start of operation: 1000 hours.

The entire former Jewish quarter was swept again today by the same assault
search details assigned to the same districts. My aim was to have the leaders
return to familiar streets and blocks of houses and courtyards so they could
penetrate further into the maze of bunkers and subterranean passages. The
assault search details, almost without exception, reported resistance, which
was overcome completely when gunfire was returned or the bunkers were
blown up. It is more and more evident that the turn has come for the toughest
and most resilient Jews and bandits. Several bunkers have been forced open
whose inhabitants had not gone above ground level during the entire operation. In a number of cases, the occupants of the bunkers were barely in a
condition to crawl to the surface after the bunkers had been blown up. The
captured Jews reported that many bunker inhabitants had gone mad from
the heat, smoke, and explosions.

Various Jews who had maintained a close liaison and collaborated with the
Polish terrorists were arrested. 29 Jews were arrested outside the former
Jewish quarter.

During today's operation, several blocks of houses were burned down. It is
the only method and method of last resort to force this rabble and subhumanity to the surface.

We again captured weapons, including incendiary bottles, explosives, and
large amounts of cash and foreign currency.

Today I again directed several so-called armament and defense enterprises
to immediately transfer their inventories. Jews have found refuge in these

macht und Polizei herübergewechselt sind, ausgekämmt werden
können. In einem Falle ergab sich dasselbe Bild wie schon
öfter, daß hinter dem angeblichen Riesenbetrieb fast über-
haupt keine Bestände und Werte vorhanden waren. Ein Betrieb
wurde sofort geschlossen und die Juden verlagert.

Ergebnis der heutigen Unternehmung:

30 Juden verlagert, 1 330 Juden aus Bunkern hervorgeholt und
sofort vernichtet. 362 Juden im Kampf erschossen. Insges. heute
erfaßt: 1 722 Juden. Dadurch erhöhte sich die Gesamtzahl der erfaßten Juden auf 29 186. Außerdem sind mit Wahrscheinlichkeit
in den 13 gesprengten Bunkern und durch Brände ungezählte Juden
umgekommen.

Z.Zt. sind von den erfaßten Juden keine mehr in Warschau. Der
vorgeschriebene Abtransport nach T II ist erfolgt.

Kräfte: Wie am Vortage.

Eigene Verluste: Keine.

Ende des heutigen Einsatzes um 21.45 Uhr, Fortsetzung am 27.4.43
um 9.oo Uhr.

F.d.R.:   Der ᛋᛋ- und Polizeiführer
                                       im Distrikt Warschau

                                        gez. Stroop

                                    ᛋᛋ-Brigadeführer
ᛋᛋ-Sturmbannführer.   u. Generalmajor d. Polizei

blocks of houses under the protection of helping arm the German Wehrmacht and Police. The buildings have to be swept. One case provided a familiar picture: a supposedly giant enterprise had practically no inventory, nothing of value. One enterprise was immediately closed and the Jews transferred.

Results of today's operation: 30 Jews transferred; 1,330 Jews removed from bunkers and immediately destroyed; 362 Jews shot dead in battle. Total apprehended today: 1,722 Jews. This brings the total figure of Jews apprehended to 29,186. Further, countless Jews have undoubtedly perished in 13 demolished bunkers and in the fires.

At present, none of the apprehended Jews are any longer in Warsaw. The prescribed transport to T II has been carried out.

Our forces: same as on the previous day

Our losses: none

End of today's operations at 2145 hours. To be continued on 27 April 1943 at 0900 hours.

> SS and Police Leader in the
> Warsaw District
>
> (signed) Stroop
>
> SS Major General and Major General
> of the Police

Certified copy
Jesuiter
SS Major

F e r n s c h r e i b e n

Absender: Der SS-und Polizeiführer im Distrikt Warschau

Warschau, den 27.4.1943

Az.: I ab - St/Gr - 16 07 - Tgb. Nr. 555/43 geh.

Betr.: Ghettoaktion.

An den
Höheren SS-und Polizeiführer Ost
- SS-Obergruppenführer und General der Polizei Krüger -
o.V.i.A.

K r a k a u .

Verlauf der Aktion am 27.4.43, Beginn 9,oo Uhr:

Für das heute angesetzte Unternehmen wurden 24 Stoßtrupps gebildet,
die wie an einigen Tagen der vergangenen Woche das ehem.jüdische Ghetto
als kleinere Durchkämmungsstoßtrupps zu durchsuchen hatten. Diese Durchkämmungsstoßtrupps holten 780 Juden aus Bunkern hervor und erschossen bei
Widerstand 115 Juden. Beendigung dieses Unternehmens etwa 15.00 Uhr. Einige
Stoßtrupps mußten weiterhin in Tätigkeit bleiben,da sie auf neue Bunker
gestoßen waren.

Um 16.oo Uhr wurde eine besondere Kampfgruppe in Stärke von 320 Führern
und Männern für die Bereinigung eines großen Häuserblocks beiderseitig
der sog.Niskastr.im Norosten des ehem.jüd.Wohnbezirks angesetzt. Nach der
Durchsuchung wurde der gesamte Block in Brand gesetzt,nachdem er vollkommen
abgeriegelt war. Bei diesem Unternehmen wurde eine erhebliche Zahl von Juden
erfaßt. Wie immer hielten sie diese zuletzt in den sich unter der Erde
befindenden oder auf den Dachböden angebrachten Bunkern. Sie feuerten bis
zum letzten Augenblick und sprangen dann nach vorherigem Herauswerfen von
Betten, Matratzen usw. mitunter sogar aus dem 4.Stockwerk auf die Straße ,
aber erst dann, wenn ihnen durch das Feuer gar kein Ausweg mehr übrigblieb.

Insgesamt wurden heute im ehem.jüd.Wohnbezirk 2560 Juden erfaßt, davon
547 erschossen. Ausserdem kamen wie immer zahlenmässig nichtfestgestellte
Juden bei der Sprengung von Bunker bzw. durch Feuer um. Die Gesamtzahl der
bei der laufenden Aktion im ehem.jüdischen Wohnbezirk erfaßten Juden be-
trägt bis heute 31.746 .

Auf Grund eines anonymen Schreibens wurde bekannt, daß anschließend,aber
außerhalb an nordostwärtigen Teil des jüdischen Wohnbezirks sich in einem
Häuserblock Juden in größerer Zahl befinden. Auf diese Gebäude wurde ein
besonderer Stoßtrupps unter Führung von Oberleutnant d.Sch. D i e h l
angesetzt. Der Stoßtruppe stellte eine Bande in einer Stärke von etwa
120 Mann, stark bewaffnet mit Pistolen, Gewehren, lMG Handgranaten, fest,
die sich zur Wehr setzten. Es gelang , 24 Banditen im Feuerkampf zu erle-
digen, 52 Banditen wurden festgenommen. Wegen Eintritt der Dunkelheit

.∕.

Teletype Message

From: SS and Police Leader in the Warsaw District

Warsaw, 27 April 1943

Ref. No.: I ab/St/Gr. 1607—*Journal No.*: 555/43 secret

Re: Ghetto operation

To:
Higher SS and Police Leader East, SS General and General of the Police
Krueger—or deputy

Cracow

Progress report of the Ghetto operation on 27 April 1943. Start of operation:
0900 hours.

For the operation scheduled today, 24 assault units were formed. These were
to act as they did several days last week as small assault sweep detachments,
to search the former Jewish Ghetto. The assault sweep detachments removed 780 Jews from bunkers and shot 115 resistant Jews. Conclusion of
operation at 1500 hours. Several assault units had to stay in action, since
they had uncovered new bunkers.

At 1600 hours, a special battle unit of 320 officers and men was sent into
action to cleanse a large block of houses on both sides of the so-called Niska
Street in the northeastern part of the former Jewish quarter. After the search,
the entire block was sealed off and set on fire. A considerable number of Jews
were apprehended during this operation. As usual, they remained to the last
in the bunkers they had constructed underground or in attics. They fired to
the last moment and jumped to the street below—sometimes from the fourth
story—only when the flames left no other escape. First, they threw down
beds, mattresses, etc.

Today, a total of 2,560 Jews was apprehended in the former Jewish quarter
and 547 of them shot. An undetermined number of Jews perished, as usual,
in the fires or when the bunkers were blown up. The number of Jews apprehended to date in the current operation in the former Jewish quarter totals
31,746.

An anonymous letter disclosed that large numbers of Jews were to be found
in a block of buildings adjoining but outside the northeastern part of the
Jewish quarter. A special assault unit, commanded by First Lieutenant of the
Protective Police Diehl, was sent into action against this building. The assault
party discovered a gang of 120 men, heavily armed with pistols, rifles, hand
grenades, and light machine guns, who offered resistance. The unit succeeded
in liquidating 24 bandits in battle; 52 bandits were apprehended. The rest
could not be captured or destroyed because of approaching darkness. The

konnte der Rest nicht erfaßt bezw. vernichtet werden. Die Gebäudeteile
sind aber sofort umstellt worden, sodaß ein Entweichen ohne weiteres
nicht möglich ist. Forsetzung der Bereinigung am morgigen Tage. Ausserdem
wurden 17 Polen, darunter 2 poln.Polizisten , festgenommen, die von dem
Vorhandensein der Bande hätten wissen müssen. Bei diesem Unternehmen
wurden u.a. erbeutet: 3 Gewehre, 12 Pistolen, teilweise größeren Kalibers,
100 poln. Eierhandgranaten, 27 deutsche Stahlhelme, eine ganze Anzahl
deutscher Uniformstücke und -Mäntel, die sogar mit dem Band der Ostmedaille
versehen waren, weitere gefüllte lMG-Magazine, 300 Schuß Munition usw.Der
Führer des Stoßtrupps hatte es wegen der Verkleidung der Banditen in deutscher Uniform außerordentlich schwer. Er hat sich aber trotzdem mit großem
Schneid durchgesetzt. Unter den erfaßten bezw. getöteten Banditen sind mit
Bestimmtheit polnische Terroristen ermittelt. Heute gelang es u.a. auch,
einen der Gründer und Führer der jüdisch-polnischen Wehrformation zu erfassen und zu liquidieren.

Das äussere Erscheinungsbild der jetzt zur Erfassung kommenden Juden ze
dass nun die Juden an die Reihe kommen, die die Führung des ganzen Wider-
standes in den Händen hatten. Mit Beschimpfungen auf Deutschland und auf
den Führer auf den Lippen und mit Flüchen auf die deutschen Soldaten
stürzten sie sich aus den brennenden Fenstern und von den Balkonen.

Durch in die Kanalisation hinabgestiegene SS-Männer wurde festgestellt,
daß die Leichen verendeter Juden in großer Anzahl vom Wasser fortge-
schwemmt werden.

Eigene Kräfte: Von 7 - 19.00 Uhr   288 deutsche Polizei ⎫
                                             200 Trawnickimänner ⎬
                                             140 poln.Polizei   ⎭ Abspe -

               Von 19 - 7.00 Uhr   288 deutsche Polizei ⎫ dienst.
                                             250 Waffen-SS   ⎬
                                             140 poln.Polizei   ⎭

Stärke der Einsatzkräfte: 3/115 deutsche Polizei
                                             4/400 Waffen-SS
                                             1/6 TN
                                             2/30 Sipo
                                             2/21 Pioniere.

Eigene Verluste: 3 Verwundete,davon
                            2 Waffen-SS
                            1 Trawnickimann.

Ende des Unternehmens: 23.00 Uhr
Fortsetzung am 28.4.43, um 10,00 Uhr.

                                             Der SS-und Polizeiführer
                                                im Distrikt Warschau
                                                   gez. Stroop

Für die Richtigkeit: SS- Brigadeführer
                                             u.Generalmajor der Polizei

buildings, however, were immediately surrounded, so escape is not possible. The purge will continue tomorrow. Also taken into custody were 17 Poles, including 2 Polish Police, who should have known of the whereabouts of this gang. Captured during this operation were 3 rifles; 12 pistols, some of heavy caliber; 100 Polish oval hand grenades; 27 German steel helmets; parts of German uniforms and coats, some even including the ribbon of the Eastern front medal; reserve magazines for light machine guns; 300 rounds of ammunition; etc. The leader of the assault unit had an extremely difficult task with bandits disguised in German uniforms. He nonetheless pushed ahead with great energy. Polish terrorists were identified with certainty among the bandits who were apprehended or killed. We even succeeded in apprehending and liquidating one of the founder-leaders of the Jewish-Polish defense formation.[18]

The external appearance of the Jews who are now being apprehended shows that the turn has come for those Jews who directed the resistance. Plunging from burning windows and balconies, they reviled Germany and the Fuehrer and cursed the German Army.

SS men who descended into the sewers discovered that a large number of Jewish corpses were being washed away.

Our forces:

From 0700 to 1900 hours	288 German Police
	200 Trawniki men
	140 Polish Police
	Blockade forces
From 1900 to 0700 hours	288 German Police
	250 Waffen-SS
	140 Polish Police
Strength of assault forces	3 officers/115 German Police
	4 officers/400 Waffen-SS
	1 officer / 6 Technical Emergency Corps
	2 officers/ 21 Engineers

Our losses: 3 wounded, including 2 Waffen-SS men and 1 Trawniki man

End of operations at 2300 hours. To be continued on 28 April 1943 at 1000 hours.

SS and Police Leader in the
Warsaw District

(signed) Stroop

SS Major General and Major General
of the Police

Certified copy
Jesuiter
SS Major

F e r n s c h r e i b e n

───

Absender: Der SS-und Polizeiführer im Distrikt Warschau

───

Warschau, den 28.4.1943

Az.: I ab- St/Gr - 16 07 Tgb.Nr. 562/43 geh.
Betr.: Ghettoaktion.

An den
Höheren SS-und Polizeiführer Ost
- SS-Obergruppenführer und General der Polizei Krüger =
o.V.i.A.

K r a k a u.

Verlauf der Aktion am 28.4.1943, Beginn 10,oo Uhr.:

Zur Durchkämmung des Gesamtghettos wurden heute 10 Stoßtrupps angesetzt. Diese Stoßtrupps stellten in zäher Kleinarbeit wiederum eine
ganze Anzahl von Bunkern fest, in denen sich die Juden, wie jetzt
festgestellt wurde, schon seit Mitte vorigen Jahres zum Widerstand
eingerichtet hatten. Insgesamt wurden 335 Juden mit Gewalt aus diesen Bunkern hervorgeholt. Neben diesen Unternehmungen wurde das Nest
der jüdischen militärischen Organisation am Rande des Ghettos weiter in Angriff genommen. Es gelang, ausser den gestern gefaßten Banditen heute weitere 10 Banditen zu erschießen, 9 festzunehmen und weitere Waffen, Munition und militärische Ausrüstungsgegenstände zu
erbeuten.

Am Nachmittag wurde eine Kampfgruppe nochmals auf einen schon durch-
kämmten Häuserblock angesetzt und dieser im Verlauf dieser Unternehmung in Brand gesetzt. Wie an den Vortagen kamen auch heute die Juden
unter der Gewalt des Feuers und der ungeheuren Rauchschwaden in Massen
zum Vorschein. An einer anderen Stelle wurde von dem seitens der Wehrmacht zugeteilten Pionieroffizier in zäher Arbeit ein Bunker geöffnet,
der seit Oktober v.J. eingerichtet und mit Wasserleitung,Klosett und
elektr.Lichtleitungen und sonstigen Zubehör ausgestattet war, wurden
274 der einflußreichsten und reichsten Juden herausgezogen.

Auch heute wurde an verschiedenen Stellen heftiger Widerstand mit
Waffengewalt festgestellt und gebrochen. Es ergibt sich nunmehr immer
klarer, daß infolge der längeren Dauer der Aktion die wirklichen
Terroristen und Aktivisten getroffen werden.

Ergebnis des heutigen Tages: 1 655 Juden zur Verlagerung erfaßt,
davon 110 im Kampf erschossen.

Weiter verbrannten viele Juden im Feuer bzw. wurde eine nicht feststellbare Anzahl von Juden durch Sprengungen in den einzelnen Bunkern
vernichtet.

                                                          b.w.

Copy

Teletype Message

From: SS and Police Leader in the Warsaw District

Warsaw, 28 April 1943

Ref. No.: I ab/St/Gr. 1607—*Journal No.*: 562/43 secret

Re: Ghetto operation

To:
Higher SS and Police Leader East, SS General and General of the Police
Krueger—or deputy

Cracow

Progress report of the Ghetto operation on 28 April 1943. Start of operation:
1000 hours.

Today, 10 assault units were dispatched to sweep the entire Ghetto. Proceeding with thoroughness and tenacity, these assault units again located a large
number of bunkers. We have now established that the Jews had prepared these
bunkers for resistance as early as the middle of last year. A total of 335 Jews
was forcibly removed from these bunkers. Besides these undertakings, we
tackled the stronghold of the Jewish military organization, which is situated
at the edge of the Ghetto. We succeeded today in shooting 10 bandits in
addition to those caught yesterday, in apprehending 9, and in capturing more
weapons, ammunition, and military equipment.

In the afternoon, a battle detail was once more dispatched against a block of
buildings that had already been swept; the block was set on fire in the course
of this undertaking. As on previous days, the powerful fire and massive smoke
forced masses of Jews out into the open. Elsewhere, an Engineer officer
assigned by the Wehrmacht worked tenaciously to open a bunker that had
been prepared last October and was equipped with running water, toilet,
electricity, and other conveniences. 274 of the most influential and richest
Jews were removed.

Today, strenuous armed resistance was again encountered and overcome at
various locations. It is now clearer than ever that due to the extended duration
of the operation, the real terrorists and activists are being struck.

Today's results: 1,655 Jews apprehended for transfer, including 110 killed
in battle.

Further, many Jews burned to death in the fires, and an indeterminable number of Jews were destroyed when several bunkers were demolished.

Durch die **Erfolge** des heutigen **Tages** erhöht sich die Zahl der insgesamt erfaßten bzw. vernichteten Juden auf 33.401. In dieser Zahl sind die verbrannten und in den Bunkern vernichteten Juden nicht erfaßt.

Eigene Kräfte: wie am Vortage.
Verluste: 3 Verwundete (davon 1 Polizei, 2 Waffen-SS).
Ende der Aktion: 22,oo Uhr. Fortsetzung am 29.4.43, 10,oo Uhr.

Der SS-und Polizeiführer
im Distrikt Warschau

gez.Stroop

SS-Brigadeführer
u. Generalmajor der Polizei.

Für die Richtigkeit:

[signature]

SS-Sturmbannführer

1061 PS

Today's success raises the total number of Jews apprehended or destroyed to 33,401. This figure does not include the Jews who burned to death or were destroyed in the bunkers.

Our forces: same as on the previous day

Our losses: 1 Police and 2 Waffen-SS wounded

End of operations at 2200 hours. To be continued on 29 April 1943 at 1000 hours.

SS and Police Leader in the
Warsaw District

(signed) Stroop

SS Major General and Major General
of the Police

Certified copy
Jesuiter
SS Major

F e r n s c h r e i b e n

Absender: Der SS-und Polizeiführer im Distrikt Warschau

Warschau, den 29.4.1943

Az.: I ab - St/Gr - 16 07 - Tgb.Nr. 566/43 geh.
Betr.:Ghettoaktion.

An den
Höheren SS-und Polizeiführer Ost
- SS-Obergruppenführer und General der Polizei Krüger
o.V.i.A.
K r a k a u .

Verlauf der Großaktion am 29.4.43, Beginn 10 Uhr:

Wie am Vortage Ansetzung von Durchkämmungsstoßtrupps,die insbesondere
die frisch abgetrennten Häuserblocks zu durchsuchen hatten.
Eine größere Kampfgruppe wurde angesetzt zur Säuberung eines Häuserblocks (ehem. Betrieb Hallmann) und zur Vernichtung dieses Blocks
durch Feuer. Insgesamt wurden 36 neue Wohnbunker festgestellt ,aus
diesen und sonstigen Verstecken sowie aus den brennenden Häusern
2 359 Juden erfaßt, davon 106 im Kampf getötet.

Erbeutet wurden wiederum: 2 Gewehre, 10 Pistolen, 10 kg Sprengstoff
und Munition verschiedener Art.

Bei der Sprengung eines großen Bunkers, bei dem das gesamte Gebäude
einstürzte, kamen die Banditen restlos um. Bei dem sich dann entwickelnden Feuer zeigten große Detonationen und Stichflammen,daß größere
Bestände an Munition und Sprengstoff vorhanden gewesen sein müssen.
Einige Kanalschächte wurden gesprengt. 2 ausserhalb des Ghettos ermittelte
Ausgänge wurden ebenfalls durch Sprengung bzw. Vermauerung unbrauchbar
gemacht.

Aus den Aussagen verschiedener Bunkerbesatzungen geht hervor,daß diese
Juden bereits 10 Tage nicht mehr aus denselben hervorgekommen sind und
daß ihnen nun infolge der längeren Dauer der Großaktion die Lebensmittel
usw. ausgehen. Weiter erklären die Juden, daß in der Nacht jüdische oder
auch polnische Banditen, die schwarze Masken trügen, erschienen und die
Bunker von außen vermauerten mit dem Hinweis,daß sie auf keinen Fall
sich melden sollen, damit sie nachher weiter im Ghetto wohnen können,Die
Räumung einiger Rüstungsbetriebe geht nur langsam vor sich. In manchen
Fällen hat es den Anschein, als geschieht dies absichtlich. So habe ich
festgestellt, daß in einem Betrieb (Schulz & Co.) ,den ich am 2.Osterfeier-
tag besichtigte und daraufhin die Anweisung gab,sofort mit der Räumung
zu beginnen, und zwar innerhalb 3 Tagen, bis heute, Donnerstag ,noch nichts
geschehen war.

                                                                b.w.

Copy

Teletype Message

From: SS and Police Leader in the Warsaw District

Warsaw, 29 April 1943

Ref. No.: I ab/St/Gr. 1607—*Journal No.*: 566/43 secret

Re: Ghetto operation

To:
Higher SS and Police Leader East, SS General and General of the Police Krueger—or deputy

Cracow

Progress report of the grand operation on 29 April 1943. Start of operation: 1000 hours.

As on the previous day, assault sweep detachments were charged with the search of the newly separated blocks of buildings. A larger battle detail was dispatched to purge a block of houses (the former Hallmann enterprise[19]) and destroy it by fire. Altogether, 36 new bunkers were located; 2,359 Jews were apprehended from these and other hideouts and from burning buildings. Of these, 106 were killed in battle.

Once again captured were 2 rifles, 10 pistols, 10 kilograms of explosives, and various types of ammunition.

When a large bunker was blown up, the entire building collapsed and the bandits perished without exception. In the ensuing blaze, loud detonations and jets of fire showed that large stores of ammunitions and explosives must have been present. Several sewer shafts were blown up. Two exits discovered outside the Ghetto were also demolished or walled up to make them useless.

Statements made by various bunker crews revealed that these Jews have not been outside for the last 10 days and that they are running short on food, etc., due to the extended duration of the grand operation. The Jews also explained that Jewish or perhaps Polish bandits wearing black masks show up at night to wall up the bunkers from outside. They urge those inside not to give any signs of life if they wish to continue living in the Ghetto. The evacuation of several armament enterprises is proceeding at a slow pace. In some cases, it would appear to be almost intentional. Thus, I discovered today, Thursday, that there has been no move by one firm (Schultz & Co.) to comply with my orders to start immediate evacuation, which I had issued during my visit there on Easter Monday, three days ago.

Eigene Kräfte: wie am Vortage.

Eigene Verluste: keine.

Ende des Unternehmens um 21 Uhr. Fortsetzung der Großaktion am 30.4.1943 , 9,oo Uhr.

Insgesamt erfaßt bzw. vernichtet: 35 760.

Der SS-und Polizeiführer
im Distrikt Warschau

gez. Stroop

SS- Brigadeführer
u. Generalmajor der Polizei

F.f.R.:

SS-Sturmbannführer

Our forces: same as on the previous day

Our losses: none

End of operations at 2100 hours. The grand operation will be continued on 30 April 1943 at 0900 hours.

Total number of Jews apprehended or destroyed: 35,760

SS and Police Leader in the
Warsaw District

(signed) Stroop

SS Major General and Major General
of the Police

Certified copy
Jesuiter
SS Major

F e r n s c h r e i b e n

Absender: Der SS-und Polizeiführer im Distrikt Warschau

Warschau, den 30.4.1943

Az.: I ab- St/Gr - 16 07 - Tgb.Nr. 579/43 geh.

Betr.: Ghettogroßaktion.

An den
Höheren SS-und Polizeiführer Ost
- SS-Obergruppenführer und General der Polizei Krüger
o.V.i.A.

K r a k a u .

Verlauf der Großaktion am 30.4.43, Beginn 9,oo Uhr.

Mit der Durchkämmung mittels Durchkämmungsstoßtrupps wurde heute fort-
gefahren. Obwohl riesige Häuserblocks bis jetzt vollkommen ausgebrannt
sind, halten sich die Juden in den 2 - 3 m sich unter der Erde befindenden Bunkern weiter auf. In vielen Fällen ist es nur möglich,diese Bunker
zu finden, wenn ein bereits gefaßter Jude irgend einen Hinweis gibt. Es
wurde durch Aussagen von Juden, die sich in den letzten Tagen wieder-
holten, festgestellt, daß nachts bewaffnete Juden aus irgend einem
Schlupfwinkel oder Bunker hervorkommen und die Juden mit Erschießen be-
drohen, wenn sie sich irgendwie bemerkbar machen. Es konnte einwandfrei
festgestellt werden, daß mehrere Bunker von aussen von den Banditen ver-
schlossen wurden, um hierdurch ihrer Anordnung Nachdruck zu geben. Insgesamt wurden heute 30 Bunker festgestellt, geleert und gesprengt. Wiederum
wurde eine große Anzahl an Banditen und Untermenschen mit erfaßt. Neben
der Durchkämmungsaktion durch kleinere Stoßtrupps waren 2 grössere Kampfgruppen auf verschiedene zusammenhängende Häuserblocks zur Durchkämmung
und Vernichtung durch Feuer angesetzt.

Insgesamt wurden heute 1 599 Juden erfaßt, davon 179 in Kampf erschossen.
Damit erhöht sich die Gesamtzahl der bisher erfaßten Juden auf 37 359.
Verladen wurden heute 3 855 Juden. Bei den in den letzten Tagen erfaßten
Juden ist die Zahl der bewaffneten erheblich gestiegen. So wurden heute
wieder Waffen und insbesondere auch deutsche Uniformstücke bei den Juden
erbeutet. Das außerdem heute angesetzte Unternehmen im Fort Traugutta ist
negativ verlaufen. Soweit unterirdische Ausgänge ermittelt werden konnten,
sind diese entweder besetzt oder gesprengt worden. Zur Bekämpfung eines
Gebäudes mußte heute ein Geschütz herangezogen werden.

Eigene Kräfte (Einsatzkräfte):	Polizei	5/133
	Sipo	3/36
	Waffen-SS	6/432
	Pioniere	2/40
	Stab	3/7

Absperrkräfte:	Waffen -SS	3/318
	Deutsche Pol.	2/89
	Trwaniçki	200, außerdem poln. Polizei

.../.

47

Teletype Message

From: SS and Police Leader in the Warsaw District

Warsaw, 30 April 1943

Ref. No.: I ab/St/Gr. 1607—*Journal No.*: 579/43 secret

Re: Grand operation in the Ghetto

To:
Higher SS and Police Leader East, SS General and General of the Police Krueger—or deputy

Cracow

Progress report of the grand operation on 30 April 1943. Start of operation: 0900 hours.

Today, assault sweep detachments continued the sweep. Although huge blocks of buildings are now completely burned out, the Jews continue to remain in bunkers located 2 to 3 meters below ground. Often we are able to find these bunkers only when an apprehended Jew tips us off. During the last few days, repeated testimony from Jews has established that armed Jews emerge at night from some hideout or bunker who threaten to shoot Jews who attract attention in any way. It was incontrovertibly established that several bunkers were sealed from the outside by these bandits to underline their orders. Today, a total of 30 bunkers was located, emptied, and blown up. Again, a large number of bandits and subhumans were apprehended. Besides the sweep operations conducted by smaller assault detachments, 2 larger battle details were dispatched to sweep and destroy by fire various contiguous housing blocks.

A total of 1,599 Jews was apprehended today, including 179 killed in battle. The total number of Jews apprehended to date thus rises to 37,359. Today, 3,855 Jews were loaded for shipment. The proportion of armed Jews has risen considerably among those apprehended during the last few days. Today, weapons and especially parts of German uniforms were again captured from the Jews. The results of today's undertaking in Fort Traugutta[20] were negative. Any subterranean exits located were occupied or blown up. A cannon had to be brought up to join in the combat against one of the buildings today.

Our combat forces:

Police	5 officers/133 men
Security Police	3 officers/ 36 men
Waffen-SS	6 officers/432 men
Engineers	2 officers/ 40 men
Staff	3 officers/ 7 men

Blockade forces:

Waffen-SS	3 officers/310 men
German Police	2 officers/ 89 men
Trawniki	200 men
In addition, Polish Police	

Eigene Verluste: 1 Verwundeter (Schutzpolizei)

Ende der heutigen Großaktion: 21 Uhr .Fortsetzung am
1.5.1943,9.oo Uhr.

                       Der SS-und Polizeiführer
                         im Distrikt Warschau

                           gez. Stroop

                       SS-Brigadeführer
                  und Generalmajor der Polizei

Für die Richtigkeit:

SS-Sturmbannführer

Our losses: 1 wounded (Protective Police)

End of today's grand operation at 2100 hours. To be continued on 1 May 1943 at 0900 hours.

> SS and Police Leader in the
> Warsaw District
>
> (signed) Stroop
>
> SS Major General and Major General
> of the Police

Certified copy
Jesuiter
SS Major

F e r n s c h r e i b e n

Absender: Der SS-und Polizeiführer im Distrikt Warschau

Warschau, den 1.Mai 1943

Az.: I ab. - St/Gr. 16 07 - Tgb.Nr. 583/43 geh.
Betr.: Ghetto-Großaktion

An den
Höheren SS-und Polizeiführer Ost
SS-Obergruppenführer und General d.Polizei Krüger
o.V.i.A.

K r a k a u .

Verlauf der Großaktion am 1.5.1943, Beginn 9.00 Uhr:

Ansetzung von 10 Durchkämmungsstoßtrupps,außerdem Ansetzung einer
größeren Kampfgruppe zur Durchkämmung eines Häuserblocks mit dem
weiteren Auftrag, diesen Häuserblock durch Brand zu vernichten. In
diesem Häuserblock befand sich ebenfalls ein sog. Rüstungsbetrieb,
der, obwohl Zeit genug vorhanden, noch nicht ganz geräumt war. Er wurde
in die Durchführung des Auftrages mit einbezogen.

Bei den heute angesetzten Unternehmungen wurden insgesamt 1.026 Juden
erfaßt, davon 245 in Kampf bzw. bei Widerstand getötet. Auch wurden eine
große Anzahl ausgesprochener Banditen und Rädelsführer gefangen. In einem
Falle gab ein bereits zum Abtransport bereitgestellter Jude 3 Schuß auf einen
Polizeioberleutnant ab, die jedoch fehlgingen. Die heute erfaßten Juden
wurden restlos nur mit Gewalt aus Bunkern hervorgeholt. Irgendwelche
freiwillige Meldungen aus den geöffneten Bunkern waren heute nicht zu verzeichnen. Eine größere Anzahl der erfaßten Juden wurde aus der Kanalisation herausgeholt. Die systematische Sprengung bzw.Verschüttung der
Kanalausgänge wurde fortgesetzt.

In einem Falle hatten die Pioniere eine stärkere geballte Ladung angelegt
und mußten zu einer Nachbaröffnung gehen, um dort irgendwelche Verrich-
tungen vorzunehmen. Inzwischen war 1 Jude aus dem Kanal hervorgestoßen,
hatte die Zündung von der geballten Ladung entfernt und diese entwendet.
Es gelang im weiteren Verfolg dieses Teilunternehmens,den Juden später
mit der geballten Ladung zu fassen.

Um die Bewegungen der Juden in der Nacht festzustellen, habe ich heute
erstmalig 5 Spähtrupps in Stärke von je 1/9 für die Dauer der Nacht in
unregelmäßigen Abständen angesetzt.

Allgemein ist festzustellen, daß die Auffindung der sich noch in sog.
Bunkern, Höhlen und im Kanalnetz befindenden Juden äußerste Aufmerksam-
keit und Anstrengung seitens der eingesetzten Männer bedarf. Es ist zu

Teletype Message

From: SS and Police Leader in the Warsaw District

Warsaw, 1 May 1943
Ref. No.: I ab/St/Gr. 1607—*Journal No.*: 583/43 secret

Re: Grand operation in the Ghetto

To:
Higher SS and Police Leader East, SS General and General of the Police
Krueger—or deputy

Cracow

Progress report of the grand operation on 1 May 1943. Start of operation: 0900 hours.

10 assault sweep detachments were sent into action; further a larger battle detail to sweep a housing block was dispatched with orders to destroy this block by fire. This block, too, contained a so-called armament enterprise that had not been completely evacuated, although there had been adequate time. It was encompassed in the execution of the mission.

Today's undertaking yielded a total of 1,026 Jews, of whom 245 were killed either in battle or while resisting. Moreover, a large number of outright bandits and ring leaders were caught. In one case, a Jew who had already been processed for deportation fired 3 shots at a First Lieutenant of Police; however, the bullets missed their mark. All the Jews apprehended today were removed from the bunkers by force. There was not a single case of voluntary surrender when the bunkers were opened. A large number of the Jews were apprehended in the sewer network. We continued to systematically blow up or plug the sewer exits.

In one case, the Engineers laid a concentrated charge and had to move to an adjacent opening to attend to some other matter. In the meantime, a Jew emerged from the sewer, removed the fuse, and stole the explosives. At a later stage in the pursuit of this part of the undertaking, we succeeded in catching the Jew with the explosives.

To establish the nightly movement of Jews, I assigned, for the first time, 5 reconnaissance details of 1 officer and 9 men each for night duty at irregular intervals.

It is a fact, generally speaking, that extraordinary diligence and energy are demanded of the troops to uncover the Jews who still are in the so-called bunkers, caves, and sewer network. We anticipate that the remaining in-

erwarten, daß nunmehr die Reste der ehemaligen Insassen des Ghettos erfaßt werden. Die Gesamtzahl der bisher erfaßten Juden hat sich auf 38 385 erhöht. Nicht einbegriffen sind die verbrannten und in den Bunkern umgekommenen Juden. Ein Stoßtrupp stellte fest, daß in einem Hauptkanal unter dem Ghetto eine nicht festzustellende Anzahl von Leichen schwammen.

Außerhalb des Ghettos in der näheren Umgebung der Stadt Warschau wurden durch Gendarmerie seit Beginn der Großaktion 150 Juden erschossen, die nachweislich aus Warschau geflüchtet waren

Erbeutet wurden wiederum Pistolen und Sprengstoff.

Eigene Kräfte:

Einsatzkräfte:	Deutsche Polizei	4/102
	Waffen-SS	7/350
	Pioniere (Wehrm.)	2/38
	TN	1/6
	Sipo	2/1

Absperrkräfte:	Waffen-SS	300
	Deutsche Polizei	1/71
	Trawnicki	250

Eigene Verluste: 1 Angeh. d.Orpo – gestern verwundet –
ist seinen Verletzungen erlegen.

Ende der heutigen Großaktion: 22,oo Uhr. Fortsetzung am 2.5.1943, 10,oo Uhr.

Der SS-und Polizeiführer
im Distrikt Warschau

gez. Stroop

SS-Brigadeführer
u. Generalmajor der Polizei

Für die Richtigkeit:

SS-Sturmbannführer

habitants of the former Ghetto will be apprehended shortly. The total figure of Jews apprehended to date has now risen to 38,385. Not included are the Jews who burned to death or perished in the bunkers. One assault unit discovered that an indeterminable number of corpses were floating in a sewer main below the Ghetto.

Outside the Ghetto, in the immediate vicinity of the city of Warsaw, the Gendarmerie has shot 150 Jews since the start of the grand operation; there is proof that these Jews had escaped from Warsaw.

Pistols and explosives were again captured.

Our combat forces:

German Police	4 officers/102 men
Waffen-SS	7 officers/350 men
Engineers (Wehrmacht)	2 officers/ 38 men
Technical Emergency Corps	1 officer / 6 men
Security Police	2 officers/ 1 man

Blockade forces:

Waffen-SS	300 men
German Police	1 officer / 71 men
Trawniki	250 men

Our losses: 1 member of the Order Police, wounded yesterday, succumbed to his injuries.

End of today's grand operation at 2200 hours. To be continued on 2 May 1943 at 1000 hours.

SS and Police Leader in the
Warsaw District

(signed) Stroop

SS Major General and Major General
of the Police

Certified copy
Jesuiter
SS Major

F e r n s c h r e i b e n   -Abschrift.

Absender: Der SS-und Polizeiführer im Distrikt Warschau.

Warschau, den 2.Mai 1943

Az.: I ab. - St/Gr - 16 07 - Tgb. Nr. 584/ 43 geh.
Betr.: Ghetto-Großaktion

An den

Höheren SS-und Polizeiführer Ost
SS-Obergruppenführer und Generald.Polizei Krüger
o.V.i.A.

K r a k a u

Verlauf der Großaktion am 2.5.43 Beginn 10.oo Uhr:

Durchkämmung des gesamten Gebietes des ehem.Ghettos durch 9 Stoßtrupps ,außerdem Ansetzung einer größeren Abteilung zur Säuberung
bzw. Vernichtung eines Häuserblocks, der sich um die beiden Rüstungsbetriebe Transavia und Wischniewski gruppiert. Die Stoßtrupps nahmen,
um neue Bunker festzustellen, zu ihren Unternehmungen am Vortage gefaßte
Juden mit, die als Wegweiser dienten. Diese Unternehmungen der Durchkämmungsstoßtrupps brachten 944 Juden aus Bunkern hervor, erschossen
wurden bei dieser Gelegenheit weitere 235 Juden. Bei der Vernichtung des
vorgenannten Häuserblocks wurden 120 Juden erfaßt und ungezählte Juden,
die infolge des Brandes aus dem Dachgeschoß auf die inneren Höfe abspran-
gen, vernichtet. Weiter sind viele Juden in den Flammen umgekommen bzw.
wurden eine weitere Anzahl von Juden durch vorgenommene Sprengungen von
Bunkern und Kanalöffnungen ebenfalls vernichtet. 2 Rüstungsbetrieben
wurden die Juden entzogen und die Betriebsführer aufgefordert,innerhalb
einer kurzfristigen Zeit zu räumen.

Insgesamt wurden am heutigen Tage erfaßt   1. 852 Juden.
Die Gesamtzahl der erfaßten Juden erhöht sich
damit auf   40.237   "

Es wurden 27 Bunker festgestellt,gewaltsam geöffnet und zerstört,
Waffen und Munition erbeutet. Durch Beschießung der äusseren Absperrung
und durch den Angriff aus einer Kanalöffnung außerhalb des ehem.jüdischen
Wohnbezirks ausbrechender Juden sind insgesamt 7 Ausfälle entstanden,davon
4 Orpo und 3 poln. Polizisten. Die in der Nacht angesetzten Spähtrupps
der Waffen-SS fanden teilweise bewaffneten Widerstand,bei den sich aus
den Löchern und Bunkern unter dem Schutze der Dunkelheit hervorwagenden
Juden. Eigene Verluste traten hierbei nicht ein. Dagegen wurde eine grössere
Anzahl von Juden erschossen bzw. verwundet.

b.w.

Teletype Message

From: SS and Police Leader in the Warsaw District

Warsaw, 2 May 1943

Ref. No.: I ab/St/Gr. 1607—*Journal No.*: 584/43 secret

Re: Grand operation in the Ghetto

To:
Higher SS and Police Leader East, SS General and General of the Police
Krueger—or deputy

Cracow

Progress report of the grand operation on 2 May 1943. Start of operation:
1000 hours.

Sweep of the entire territory of the former Ghetto was conducted by 9 assault
detachments; a larger detachment was further detailed to purge and/or
destroy a housing block grouped around the 2 armament works, Transavia
and Wisniewski.[21] To locate new bunkers, the assault detachments took along
as guides Jews who had been apprehended the day before. The assault sweep
detachments removed 944 Jews from bunkers during the course of this undertaking; an additional 235 Jews were shot. When the abovementioned housing
block was destroyed, 120 Jews were apprehended and countless Jews destroyed when they jumped from burning attics to the inner courtyards. Many
other Jews perished in the flames or were destroyed when bunkers and sewer
entrances were blown up. Two armament concerns were deprived of their
Jews and the plant managers requested to complete evacuation within a
brief span of time.

Altogether, 1,852 Jews were apprehended today. The total number of Jews
apprehended thereby rises to 40,237.

27 bunkers were located, forcibly opened, and destroyed; arms and ammunition were captured. There was a total of 7 casualties, consisting of 4 Order
Police and 3 Polish Police. These occurred when the outer barricade came
under fire and when Jews attacked while breaking out through a sewer
entrance outside the former Jewish quarter. The Waffen-SS reconnaissance
detachments assigned during the night met some armed resistance from Jews
who ventured out of manholes and bunkers under the protection of darkness.
We suffered no losses. A considerable number of Jews, on the other hand,
were killed or wounded.

Eigene Kräfte.

Einsatzkräfte: Deutsche Polizei   3/98
                        TN   1/6
                        Sicherheitspolizei   3/12
                        Pioniere (Wehrm.)   2/37
                        SS-Gren.u.)   11/409
                        Kavallerie)   3/7

Absperrkräfte: Deutsche Polizei   2/9
                        SS-Grenadiere   1/300
                        Trawnicki   200..

Eigene Verluste: 4 Orpo verwundet,
                        3 poln.Polizei verwundet.

Der heutigen Großaktion wohnte der Höhere SS-und Polizeiführer
Ost, SS-Obergruppenführer und General der Polizei K r ü g e r, bei.

Ende der Aktion : 20,3o Uhr. Fortsetzung am 3.5.43, 9.oo Uhr.

                                    Der SS-und Polizeiführer
                                    im Distrikt Warschau

                                    gez. Stroop

                                    SS- Brigadeführer
                                u. Generalmajor der Polizei

Für die Richtigkeit:

SS-Sturmbannführer

Our forces:

Sent into action

German Police	3 officers/ 98 men
Technical Emergency Corps	1 officer / 6 men
Security Police	3 officers/ 12 men
Engineers	2 officers/ 37 men
SS Grenadiers	11 officers/409 men
SS Cavalry	3 officers/ 7 men

Blockade forces

German Police	2 officers/ 9 men
SS Grenadiers	1 officer /300 men
Trawniki	200 men

Our losses: 4 Order Police and 3 Polish Police wounded

The Higher SS and Police Leader East, SS General and General of the Police Krueger, attended today's grand operation.

End of operations at 2030 hours. To be continued on 3 May 1943 at 0900 hours.

> SS and Police Leader in the
> Warsaw District
>
> (signed) Stroop
>
> SS Major General and Major General
> of the Police

Certified copy
Jesuiter
SS Major

F e r n s c h r e i b e n

Absender: Der SS und Polizeiführer im Distrikt Warschau

Warschau, den 3.Mai 1943

Az.: I ab- Str/Gr. - 16 07 - Tgb. Nr. 597/43 geh.

Betr.: Ghetto-Großaktion.

An den
Höheren SS-und Polizeiführer Ost
SS-Obergruppenführer und General d.Polizei Krüger
o.V.i.A.
K r a k a u

Verlauf der Großaktion am 3.5.43 , Beginn 9,oo Uhr:

Die Durchkämmung des ehem.jüdischen Ghettos am heutigen Tage, bei der
wiederum 19 Bunker ermittelt wurden, hatte folgendes Ergebnis:

Aus Bunkern erfaßt	1.392	Juden
erschossen	95	"
aus ehem.Rüstungsbetrieben umgelagert	177	"
Dadurch erhöht sich die Gesamtzahl der bisher		
erfaßten Juden auf	41.806	"

In den meisten Fällen leisteten die Juden mit der Waffe in der Hand
vor Verlassen des Bunkers Widerstand. Dadurch sind 2 Ausfälle durch
Verwundung zu verzeichnen. Die Juden und Banditen feuerten teilweise
mit beiden Händen aus Pistolen.

Da heute in mehreren Fällen festgestellt wurde, daß Jüdinnen Pistolen in
ihren Schlüpfern verborgen hatten, wurden ab heute sämtliche Juden und
Banditen aufgefordert, sich restlos zur Durchsuchung zu entkleiden.

Erbeutet wurden u.a. 1 deutsches Gewehr, Modell 98, 2 Pistolen 08 und
andere Kaliber, weiter selbstgefertigte Handgranaten. Erst nach Abbrennen
von mehreren Nebelkerzen sind die Juden zum Verlassen ihrer Bunker zu
bewegen. Nach gestern und heute gemachten Aussagen wurden im letzten
Halbjahr 1942 die Juden aufgefordert, Luftschutzkeller zu bauen. Unter
der Tarnung , Luftschutzkeller zu bauen, wurde bereits damals mit dem
Bau der jetzt von den Juden bezogenen Bunker begonnen, um diese bei einer
Aktion gegen die Juden benutzen zu können.

Einige der im Ghetto angesetzten Spähtrupps wurden in der letzten
Nacht beschossen. Ein Ausfall durch Verwundung. Diese Spähtrupps
meldeten, daß bewaffnete Banditen in Gruppen durch das ehem. Ghetto
marschierten.

Kräfte: wie am Vortage.

.⁄.

Copy

Teletype Message

From: SS and Police Leader in the Warsaw District

Warsaw, 3 May 1943

Ref. No.: I ab/St/Gr. 1607—*Journal No.*: 597/43 secret

Re: Grand operation in the Ghetto

To:
Higher SS and Police Leader East, SS General and General of the Police
Krueger—or deputy

Cracow

Progress report of the grand operation on 3 May 1943. Start of operation:
0900 hours.

Today's sweep of the former Jewish Ghetto, during which 19 new bunkers
were discovered, had the following results:

Apprehended in bunkers	1,392 Jews
Shot	95 Jews
Transferred from former armament enterprises	177 Jews
Total number of Jews apprehended to date	41,806 Jews

In most cases, the Jews offered resistance, weapon in hand, before leaving the
bunkers. This accounts for 2 of our men being listed as wounded. Some of
the Jews and bandits fired pistols from both hands.

Since it was established in several instances today that Jewesses had concealed
pistols in their underpants, all Jews and bandits are requested, from today on,
to strip completely and be searched.

Captured today were 1 German rifle, model 98; 2 pistols of .08 caliber and
other calibers; and homemade hand grenades. Only after the burning of
several smoke candles could the Jews be induced to leave their bunkers. According to testimony received yesterday and today, the Jews were summoned
to build air-raid shelters during the second half of 1942. Under the camouflage of constructing air-raid shelters, the Jews then began to build the
bunkers they now occupy in order to be able to make use of them during an
operation against the Jews.

Some of the reconnaissance detachments detailed to the Ghetto were fired
upon last night. One man was wounded. The reconnaissance detachments
reported that groups of armed bandits marched through the former Ghetto.

Our forces: same as on the previous day

Eigene Verluste: 3 SS-Männer verwundet.

Ende des heutigen Unternehmens: 21,00 Uhr, Fortsetzung am 4.5.43, um 9.oo Uhr.

Verladen wurden: 3 019 Juden.

                              Der SS-und Polizeiführer
                                im Distrikt Warschau

                                   gez. Stroop

                                SS- Brigadeführer
                              u. Generalmajor der Polizei

F.d.Richtigkeit:

SS-Sturmbannführer

Our losses: 3 SS Privates wounded

End of today's undertaking at 2100 hours. To be continued on 4 May 1943 at 0900 hours.

Loaded for shipment were 3,019 Jews.

> SS and Police Leader in the
>   Warsaw District
>
> (signed) Stroop
>
> SS Major General and Major General
>   of the Police

Certified copy
Jesuiter
SS Major

F e r n s c h r e i b e n

Absender: Der SS-und Polizeiführer im Distrikt Warschau

Warschau, den 4.5.1943

Az.: Iab - St/Gr. - 16 07 - Tgb. Nr.603/43 geh.
Betr.: Ghetto-Großaktion

An den Höheren SS-und Polizeiführer Ost
SS-Obergruppenführer und General d.Polizei Krüger
o.V.i.A.

K r a k a u

Verlauf der Großaktion am 4.5.1943 , Beginn 9,oo Uhr:

Zur Aushebung von Bunkern wurde ein Stoßtrupp in Stärke von 1/60, der
durch das Pionierkommando der Wehrmacht verstärkt wurden, angesetzt.
Dieser Stoßtrupp brachte 550 Juden aus Bunkern und erschoß 198 Juden
im Kampf. Die Feststellung der Bunker macht immer größere Schwierigkei-
ten. Die Bunker sind oft nur durch Verrat anderer Juden aufzuspüren.
Der Aufforderung, die Bunker freiwillig zu verlassen, wird fast in keinem
Falle Folge geleistet, lediglich die immer wieder zur Anwendung kommenden Nebelkerzen zwingen die Junden dazu.

Zur Durchkämmung ,Säuberung und Vernichtung zweier großer Häuserblocks
der ehemaligen Firmen Többens,Schulz u.Co. u.a. wurden die Hauptkräfte
gegen 11.oo Uhr angesetzt. Nachdem diese Blocks vollkommen abgeriegelt
waren, wurden zunächst die sich noch darin befindenden Juden zur freiwilligen Meldung aufgefordert. Hierdurch wurden 456 Juden zur Verlagerung
erfaßt. Erst nachdem die Häuserblocks durch Feuer der Vernichtung ent-
gegengingen, kamen eine erhebliche Zahl von Juden durch das Feuer und den
Rauch gezwungen zum Vorschein. Immer wieder versuchen die Juden, selbst
durch brennende Gebäude hindurchzuwechseln. Ungezählte Juden, die sich
während der Feuersbrunst auf den Dächern zeigten, sind in den Flammen
umgekommen. Andere kamen erst im letzten Augenblick in den höchsten Stockwerken zum Vorschein und konnten sich nur durch Abspringen vor dem Verbrennungstod retten. Es wurden am heutigen Tage insgesamt 2 283 Juden erfaßt, davon 204 erschossen, ungezählte Juden in Bunkern und durch Feuer
vernichtet. Die Gesamtzahl der bisher erfaßten Juden erhöht sich auf
44.089.

Wie aus Aussagen der Juden hervorgeht, ist heute ein Teil des Kopfes
der sog. "Partei" erfaßt worden. Ein Angehöriger der Führung der Bande
wird morgen dazu verwandt, um weitere gesicherte Bunker mit bewaffneten
Insassen auszuheben. Bei der Räumung der Rüstungsbetriebe könnte erneut
festgestellt werden, daß statt des sogen. wertvollen Heeresgutes Lappalien,
wie alte Möbel und sonstige requirierte Sachen abgefahren wurden. Es wurde
sofort an Ort und Stelle dagegen eingeschritten.

.⁄.

Copy

Teletype Message

From: SS and Police Leader in the Warsaw District

Warsaw, 4 May 1943

Ref. No.: I ab/St/Gr. 1607—*Journal No.*: 603/43 secret

Re: Grand operation in the Ghetto

To:
Higher SS and Police Leader East, SS General and General of the Police
Krueger—or deputy

Cracow
Progress report of the grand operation on 4 May 1943. Start of operation:
0900 hours.

An assault detachment, 1 officer and 60 men strong, reinforced by the
Wehrmacht Engineers, was dispatched to clear out the bunkers. This assault
detachment pulled 550 Jews from bunkers and shot 188 Jews in battle.
Locating the bunkers becomes more and more difficult. Many bunkers can be
discovered only when other Jews betray their location. If Jews are ordered to
leave bunkers voluntarily, they almost never obey; they can be compelled to
do so only by the use of smoke candles.

Our main forces were dispatched about 1100 hours to sweep, purge, and
destroy 2 large housing blocks of the former firms of Toebbens, Schultz & Co.,
and others. After these blocks were completely cordoned off, the Jews who
were still in the buildings were first ordered to come forward voluntarily.
456 Jews were thereby apprehended for transfer. Only when the housing
blocks were engulfed by fire and headed for destruction did a considerable
number of Jews emerge, forced to flee the flames and smoke. Repeatedly,
the Jews tried to pass through burning buildings. Countless Jews who had
been visible on the roofs during the conflagration perished in the flames.
Others came into view on the uppermost floors at the very last moment and
could save themselves from being cremated alive only by jumping. Today, a
total of 2,283 Jews was apprehended, of whom 204 were shot; countless
Jews were destroyed in fires and in bunkers. The sum total of Jews apprehended to date has risen to 44,089.

According to testimony by the Jews, part of the leadership of the so-called
party[22] was apprehended today. One member of the leadership of the gang
will be used tomorrow to clear out other fortified bunkers and their armed
inhabitants. During the evacuation of the armament plant, it was again
established that trifles like used furniture and other requisitioned items were
carted away in place of the so-called valuable military equipment. Appropriate countermeasures were taken at once.

Die in der Nacht im ehem. jüdischen Wohnbezirk sich bewegenden Spähtrupps
meldeten erneut von Bewengungen der Juden in den abgebrannten und zertrümmerten Straßen und Höfen. Damit die Spähtrupps die Juden besser über-
raschen können, haben diese nachts ihr Schuhwerk mit Lappen und sonstigem
Material umwickelt. Bei Zusammenstößen der Spähtrupps mit Juden wurden
30 Juden erschossen.

Erbeutet wurden heute 1 Karabiner, 3 Pistolen und Munition. Bei dem
Brand explodierte eine größere Menge gelagerter Munition.

Eigene Kräfte:

Einsatzkräfte:	Deutsche Polizei	4/101
	TN	1/6
	Sipo	2/14
	Pioniere	2/41
	Waffen-SS	11/407

Absperrkräfte:	bei Tag	bei Nacht
Deutsche Pol.	2/87	1/11
Waffen SS	25	1/300
Trawnicki	200	
Poln.Polizei	1/180	1/180

Eigene Verluste: keine.

Ende des Unternehmens: 23,30 Uhr, Fortsetzung am 5.5.43 , um 10,00 Uhr.

Der SS-und Polizeiführer
im Distrikt Warschau

gez. Stroop

SS-Brigadeführer
u. Generalmajor der Polizei

Für die Richtigkeit :

SS-Sturmbannführer

Reconnaissance detachments patrolling the former Jewish quarter during the night reported renewed movement by Jews in the burned-out ruins of streets and courtyards. The reconnaissance detachments wrapped rags and other material around their foot gear at night to enable them to take the Jews by surprise. 30 Jews were shot in skirmishes with the reconnaissance detachments.

Captured today were 1 carbine, 3 pistols, and ammunition. During the blaze, a large amount of stored ammunition exploded.

Our forces:

Sent into action

German Police	4 officers/101 men
Technical Emergency Corps	1 officer / 6 men
Security Police	2 officers/ 14 men
Engineers	2 officers/ 41 men
Waffen-SS	11 officers/407 men

Blockade forces

	Day	*Night*
German Police	2 officers/ 87 men	1 officer / 11 men
Waffen-SS	25 men	1 officer /300 men
Trawniki	200 men	
Polish Police	1 officer /180 men	1 officer /180 men

Our losses: none

End of operations at 2330 hours. To be continued on 5 May 1943 at 1000 hours.

SS and Police Leader in the
Warsaw District

(signed) Stroop

SS Major General and Major General
of the Police

Certified copy
Jesuiter
SS Major

F e r n s c h r e i b e n

Absender: Der SS-und Polizeiführer im Distrikt Warschau

Warschau, den 5.5.1943

Az.: I ab.-St/Gr - 16 07 - Tgb.Nr.607/43 geh.
Betr.: Chetto-Grossaktion

An den

Höheren SS-und Polizeiführer Ost
SS-Obergruppenführer und General d.Polizei Krüger
o.V.i.A.

K r a k a u .

Verlauf der Grossaktion am 5.5.43, Beginn 10.oo Uhr:

Bei der heutigen Grossaktion hatte es zunächst den Anschein, als wenn die angesetzten Stosstrupps weniger Erfolg haben würden. Am Ende des heutigen Unternehmens
zeigte sich jedoch, dass auf Grund von Verrat und durch den
Spürsinn der Männer eine erhebliche Zahl weiterer Bunker
festgestellt wurde. Von diesen Bunkern wurden 40 zerstört.
Soweit möglich, wurden die sich in diesen Bunkern befindenden Juden erfasst /insges. 1.070/. Von den Durchkäm-
mungsstosstrupps wurden etwa 126 Juden erschossen. Auch
heute leisteten die Juden, bevor sie gefangen wurden, an
verschiedenen Stellen Widerstand. In mehreren Fällen wurden
die Öffnungen /Luken/ zu den Bunkern von innen mit Gewalt
zugehalten bzw. verriegelt, so dass nur mit einer starken
Sprengung eine Öffnung erzwungen und die Bunkerinsassen
vernichtet werden konnten. Wiederum wurden heute Waffen
und Munition erbeutet, darunter 1 Pistole 08. Aus einem
noch bestehenden Betriebe /sog. Prosta/ wurden 2 850 Juden zur Umlagerung erfasst. Diese Zahl war schon in der
bisher angegebenen Gesamterfassung enthalten, so dass sich
die Gesamtzahl um 1 070 auf 45 159 erhöht.

Eigene Kräfte: wie am Vortage.

Eigene Verluste : 1 SS-Mann verwundet, 1 Orpo verwundet.
Bisherige Gesamtverluste: 8 Tote, 55 Verwundete.
Ende der Aktion: 22.oo Uhr, Fortsetzung am 6.5.43, 9,3o Uhr

Der SS-und Polizeiführer
im Distrikt Warschau
gez. Stroop

F.d.R.

SS- Brigadeführer
u. Generalmajor der Polizei

SS-Sturmbannführer

Copy

Teletype Message

From: SS and Police Leader in the Warsaw District

Warsaw, 5 May 1943

Ref. No.: I ab/St/Gr. 1607—*Journal No.*: 607/43 secret

Re: Grand operation in the Ghetto

To:
Higher SS and Police Leader East, SS General and General of the Police Krueger—or deputy

Cracow

Progress report of the grand operation on 5 May 1943. Start of operation: 1000 hours.

At first glance, it appeared as if the assault detachments committed to today's grand operation would have less success. However, by the end of today's undertaking, a great many more bunkers had been located due to betrayal by Jews and the tracking ability of the men. 40 of these bunkers were destroyed. As far as possible, the Jews found in these bunkers were apprehended (1,070 altogether). The assault sweep detachments shot about 126 Jews. Today, the Jews again offered resistance in various places before they were caught. In several cases, the entrance hatches to the bunkers were forcibly kept closed or bolted from the inside so that only a strong explosive charge could force an opening and the bunker occupants be destroyed. Once again, weapons and ammunition were captured, including one .08-caliber pistol. 2,850 Jews were apprehended for transshipment at a still existent enterprise in the so-called Prosta.[23] Because this figure was included in the total reported earlier, only 1,070 are to be added, raising the total number to 45,159.

Our forces: same as on the previous day

Our losses: 1 SS Private and I Order Police wounded. Total losses to date: 8 dead, 55 wounded

End of operations at 2200 hours. To be continued on 6 May 1943 at 0930 hours.

> SS and Police Leader in the
> Warsaw District
>
> (signed) Stroop
>
> SS Major General and Major General
> of the Police

Certified copy
Jesuiter
SS Major

A b s c h r i f t !
F e r n s c h r e i b e n

Absender: Der ᛋᛋ- und Polizeiführer im Distrikt Warschau

Warschau, den 6.5.1943

Az.: I ab St/Gr. 16 07 - Tgb.Nr. 614/43 geh.
Betr.: Ghetto-Großaktion

An den
Höheren ᛋᛋ- und Polizeiführer Ost
ᛋᛋ-Obergruppenführer und General d. Polizei Krüger
o.V.i.A.

K r a k a u

Verlauf der Großaktion am 6.5.43, Beginn 9,30 Uhr:

Heute wurden insbesondere die Häuserblocks durchkämmt, die am 4.5. durch Feuer vernichtet wurden. Obwohl kaum zu erwarten war, daß hier noch Menschen lebend angetroffen würden, wurden eine ganze Anzahl von Bunkern, in denen sich eine glühende Hitze entwickelt hatte, festgestellt. Aus diesen Bunkern und aus in anderen Teilen des Ghettos festgestellten wurden insgesamt 1 553 Juden erfaßt. Beim Widerstand und bei einem sich entwickelnden Feuergefecht wurden 356 Juden erschossen. Bei diesem Feuergefecht schossen die Juden aus Pistolen 08 und anderen Kalibern und warfen mit poln. Eierhandgranaten. Hierbei wurde 1 ᛋᛋ-Unterscharführer verwundet. Insgesamt wurden 47 Bunker zerstört.

2 Männer der äußeren Absperrung fielen durch Verwundung aus. Anscheinend kommen die aus dem Ghetto ausgebrochenen Juden jetzt mit dem Vorsatz zurück, die Ghettojuden mit Gewalt zu entlasten bzw. zu befreien. 1 Jude, der aus Lublin entwichen war, wurde kurz vor der Ghettomauer erfaßt. Er war wie folgt bewaffnet: 1 Pistole 08, Reservemunition in größerer Anzahl, 2 poln. Eierhandgranaten. Es ist bisher nicht einwandfrei festgestellt, daß die sogen. "Parteileitung" der Juden ("PPR.") erfaßt oder vernichtet wurde. Die Spur der Banditen ist bekannt. Hoffentlich wird es bei dem morgigen Unternehmen gelingen, diese sog. Parteileitung auszuheben. Um die sich an das Ghetto herandrängenden Juden und Banditen mit größerer Sicherheit abfangen zu können, sind Sicherungen der äußeren Absperrung weiter in den arischen Teil vorgeschoben. Das ehem. Zwergghetto Prosta wurde heute durch Durchkämmungsstoßtrupps durchsucht. Es gelang die Erfassung von zurückgebliebenen Juden. Der Firma Többens wurde aufgegeben, dieses Zwergghetto bis zum 10.5.43, mittags, zu räumen. Zur vorläufigen Lagerung der Rohstoffe usw. wurde die sog. Bibliothek außerhalb des Ghettos zur Verfügung gestellt.

Die Gesamtzahl der bisher erfaßten Juden erhöht sich auf 47 068.

Copy

Teletype Message

From: SS and Police Leader in the Warsaw District

Warsaw, 6 May 1943

Ref. No.: I ab/St/Gr. 1607—*Journal No.*: 614/43 secret

Re: Grand operation in the Ghetto

To:
Higher SS and Police Leader East, SS General and General of the Police:
Krueger—or deputy

Cracow

Progress report of the grand operation on 6 May 1943. Start of operation:
0930 hours.

Today, we especially swept housing blocks that were destroyed by fire on 4
May. Although it was scarcely expected that any living beings would still be
encountered, a large number of bunkers were discovered where intense heat
had developed. A total of 1,553 Jews was apprehended in these bunkers and
in bunkers discovered in other sections of the Ghetto. 356 Jews were shot
while resisting during a skirmish. In this skirmish, Jews fired from .08-caliber
and other caliber pistols and threw Polish oval hand grenades. One SS Sergeant
was wounded. Altogether, 47 bunkers were destroyed.

Two men serving on the blockade were wounded. Apparently, Jews who had
broken out of the Ghetto were now returning with the intention of assisting
or liberating the Ghetto Jews by force. One Jew who had escaped from
Lublin[24] was apprehended just outside the Ghetto walls. He was armed with
one .08-caliber pistol, ample reserve ammunition, and 2 Polish oval hand
grenades. So far, it could not be reliably ascertained whether the so-called
Jewish party leadership (PPR) has been apprehended or destroyed. The
bandits' trail is known. It is to be hoped that tomorrow's undertaking will
succeed in clearing out this so-called party leadership. Security posts of the
surrounding barricade were moved farther into the Aryan section to more
effectively intercept the Jews and bandits who are pushing toward the Ghetto.
Prosta, the former mini-Ghetto, was searched today by assault sweep detachments. Jews who had stayed behind were apprehended. The firm of
Toebbens was charged with evacuating the mini-Ghetto by noon on 10 May
1943. The so-called library,[25] located outside the Ghetto, was placed at their
disposal for temporary storage of raw materials, etc.

Die poln. Polizei bemüht sich, angespornt durch die ausgezahlten Geldbelohnungen, jeden sich im Stadtbild zeigenden Juden bei der Befehlsstelle abzuliefern. Es gehen anonyme Briefe an den Unterzeichneten ein, in denen auf das Vorhandensein von Juden im arischen Teil aufmerksam gemacht wird. Ein anonymer Brief befaßt sich mit einem Vergleich zwischen Katyn und der Großaktion im Ghetto.

Eigene Kräfte:

Einsatzkräfte	Deutsche Polizei	4/101
	TN	1/6
	Sipo	2/14
	Pioniere (WH)	3/72
	Waffen-SS	10/500

Absperrkräfte:	bei Tag	bei Nacht
Deutsche Polizei	2/87	1/11
Waffen-SS	25	1/300
Trawniki	200	-
poln. Polizei	1/180	1/180

Eigene Verluste: 1 Orpo tot
                  1 Orpo schwer verwundet
                  1 SS-Unterscharführer leichter verwundet.

Ende der Aktion: 21.oo Uhr, Fortsetzung am 7.5.43, um 9.3o Uhr.

F.d.R.:   Der SS- und Polizeiführer
                                                  im Distrikt Warschau

                                                    gez. Stroop

SS-Sturmbannführer.   SS-Brigadeführer
                                               u.Generalmajor der Polizei

The total number of Jews apprehended so far has risen to 47,068. The Polish Police, spurred by the cash rewards, are making a great effort to deliver to headquarters any Jews found in the city. The undersigned is receiving anonymous letters that draw attention to the presence of Jews in the Aryan part of the city. One anonymous letter concerned a comparison between Katyn and the grand operation in the Ghetto.[26]

Our forces:

Sent into action

German Police	4 officers/101 men
Technical Emercency Corps	1 officer / 6 men
Security Police	2 officers/ 14 men
Engineers (Wehrmacht)	3 officers/ 72 men
Waffen-SS	10 officers/500 men

Blockade forces

	Day	*Night*
German Police	2 officers/ 87 men	1 officer / 11 men
Waffen-SS	25 men	1 officer /300 men
Trawniki	200 men	
Polish Police	1 officer /180 men	1 officer /180 men

Our losses: 1 Order Police dead; 1 Order Police wounded; 1 SS Sergeant less seriously wounded

End of operations at 2100 hours. To be continues on 7 May 1943 at 0930 hours.

> SS and Police Leader in the
> Warsaw District
>
> (signed) Stroop
>
> SS Major General and Major General
> of the Police

Certified copy
ᵔ Jesuiter
SS Major

A b s c h r i f t !
F e r n s c h r e i b e n

Absender: Der ℋ– und Polizeiführer im Distrikt Warschau

Warschau, den 7.5.43

Az.: I ab St/Gr – 16 07 – Tgb.Nr. 616/43 geh.
Betr.: Ghetto-Großaktion

An den

Höheren ℋ– und Polizeiführer Ost
ℋ–Obergruppenführer und General der Polizei Krüger
o.V.i.A.

K r a k a u

Verlauf der Großaktion am 7.5.43, Beginn 10.00 Uhr:

Die angesetzten Durchkämmungsstoßtrupps hatten heute folgende Erfolge zu verzeichnen: 49 Bunker festgestellt. Zum Teil wurden die Juden erfaßt. Eine größere nicht bekannte Zahl von Juden, die sich weigerten, die Bunker zu verlassen und bewaffneten Widerstand leistete, sind in den gesprengten Bunkern umgekommen. Insgesamt wurden heute 1 019 Juden lebend erfaßt, 255 erschossen. Die Gesamtzahl der bisher erfaßten Juden erhöht sich auf 48 342.

Heute wurde wiederum verschiedentlich auf bewaffneten Widerstand gestoßen, wobei 1 ℋ–Mann durch Verwundung ausfiel. Erbeutet wurden 4 Pistolen versch. Kalibers und Munitionsbestände.

Die Lage des Bunkers der sogen. engeren "Parteileitung" ist nunmehr bekannt. Er soll morgen mit Gewalt geöffnet werden.

Die Juden sagen aus, daß sie nachts an die frische Luft kommen, da ein ununterbrochener Aufenthalt in ihren Bunkern für sie durch die längere Dauer der Aktion unerträglich wird. Durchschnittlich werden durch die Stoßtrupps in jeder Nacht 30 – 50 Juden erschossen. Nach diesen Aussagen muß angenommen werden, daß immer noch eine größere Zahl von Juden sich unterirdisch im Ghetto aufhält. Heute wurde ein Betongebäude, das durch Feuer nicht zu vernichten war, gesprengt. Hierbei wurde festgestellt, daß das Sprengen von Häusern ungemein langwierig ist und eine Riesenmenge an Munition erfordert. Die einzige und beste Methode zur Vernichtung der Juden ist daher immer noch die Anlegung von Bränden.

Eigene Kräfte: wie am Vortage.

Eigene Verluste: 1 Angeh.d.Waffen-ℋ verwundet.

Ende der Aktion: 21.oo Uhr, Fortsetzung am 8.5.43, um 10.00 Uhr.

F.d.R.:

[signature]

ℋ–Sturmbannführer.

Der ℋ– und Polizeiführer
im Distrikt Warschau

gez. Stroop

ℋ–Brigadeführer
u.Generalmajor der Polizei

Copy

Teletype Message

From: SS and Police Leader in the Warsaw District

Warsaw, 7 May 1943

Ref. No.: I ab/St/Gr. 1607—*Journal No.*: 616/43 secret

Re: Grand operation in the Ghetto

To:
Higher SS and Police Leader East, SS General and General of the Police Krueger—or deputy

Cracow

Progress report of the grand operation on 7 May 1943. Start of operation: 1000 hours.

The assault sweep detachments sent into action today were able to record the following results: 49 bunkers located. A number of Jews were apprehended. A larger but unknown number of Jews who refused to leave the bunkers and offered armed resistance perished when the bunkers were blown up. Altogether, 1,019 Jews were apprehended alive today; 255 were shot. The total number of Jews apprehended so far has risen to 48,342.

Today, armed resistance was again encountered in several instances, whereby 1 SS Private was wounded. Four pistols of various calibers and ammunition were captured.

The location of the bunker used by the so-called inner party leadership is now known. It will be forced open tomorrow.

The Jews testify that they emerge at night to obtain fresh air, since an uninterrupted stay in the bunkers due to the long duration of the operation is becoming unbearable. On the average, the assault detachments shoot between 30 and 50 Jews each night. It must be assumed from the testimony that a considerable number of Jews still remain underground in the Ghetto. Today, a concrete building that could not be destroyed by fire was blown up. In the process, we established that the blowing up of houses is a protracted matter and requires enormous quantities of explosives. Setting fires still remains the best and only method for destroying the Jews.

Our forces: same as on the previous day

Our losses: 1 Waffen-SS man wounded

End of operations at 2100 hours. To be continued on 8 May 1943 at 1000 hours.

SS and Police Leader in the
Warsaw District

(signed) Stroop

SS Major General and Major General
of the Police

Certified copy
Jesuiter
SS Major

A b s c h r i f t !
F e r n s c h r e i b e n

Absender: Der ᛋᛋ- und Polizeiführer im Distrikt Warschau

Warschau, den 8. Mai 1943

Az.:   I ab St/Gr - 16 07 - Tgb.Nr. 624/43 geh.
Betr.: Ghetto-Großaktion

An den

Höheren ᛋᛋ- und Polizeiführer Ost
ᛋᛋ-Obergruppenführer und General der Polizei Krüger
o.V.i.A.

K r a k a u

Verlauf der Aktion am 8.5.43, 10.oo Uhr:

Das gesamte Gebiet des ehem. jüdischen Ghettos wurde heute von
Durchkammungsstoßtrupps nach vorhandenen Bunkern und Juden durchsucht. Wie schon vor einigen Tagen gemeldet, halten sich z.Zt.
noch das Untermenschentum, die Banditen und Terroristen in Bunkern auf, in denen durch die Brände die Hitze unerträglich geworden ist. Diese Kreaturen wissen nun genau, daß es nur eines gibt,
entweder sich verborgen zu halten, solange es gent oder an die
Erdoberfläche zu kommen, dabei aber den Versuch zu machen, mög-
lichst die sie bedrängenden Männer der Waffen-ᛋᛋ, der Polizei und
der Wehrmacht zu verwunden bzw. umzulegen.

Die im gestrigen FS gemeldeten Auffindung der Lager des Bunkers
der sog. engeren "Parteileitung" wurde am heutigen Tage wieter
verfolgt. Es ist gelungen, den Bunker der Parteileitung zu öffnen
und etwa 60 Banditen, die schwer bewaffnet waren, zu packen. Es
gelang, den stellv. Leiter der jüdischen militärischen Organisation "ZWZ" und seinen sog. Stabschef zu fangen und zu liquidieren.
In diesem Bunker waren etwa 200 Juden untergebracht, 60 davon
wurden erfaßt, 140 durch große Einwirkung von Nebelkerzen und
durch Anlegung großer Sprengladungen an verschiedenen Stellen
vernichtet. Durch die Nebelkerzen waren bereits ungezählte Tote
von den hervorgebrachten Juden gemeldet. Wenn der Kampf gegen
die Juden und Banditen in den ersten 6 Tagen schwer war, so muß
festgestellt werden, daß nunmehr die Juden und Jüdinnen erfaßt
werden, die die Träger des Kampfes dieser Tage waren. Es wird
kein Bunker mehr geöffnet, ohne daß von den darin sich befindenden Juden mit den innen zur Verfügung stehenden Waffen, lMG.,
Pistolen und Handgranaten Widerstand geleistet wird. Heute wurden wiederum eine ganze Anzahl Jüdinnen erfaßt, die in ihren
Schlüpfern entsicherte und geladene Pistolen trugen.

Nach gemachten Aussagen sollen sich noch etwa 3 - 4000 Juden in
den unterirdischen Löchern, Kanälen und Bunkern aufhalten. Der
Unterzeichnete ist entschlossen, die Großaktion nicht eher zu be-

Copy

Teletype Message

From: SS and Police Leader in the Warsaw District

Warsaw, 8 May 1943

Ref. No.: I ab/St/Gr. 1607—*Journal No.*: 624/43 secret

Re: Grand operation in the Ghetto

To:
Higher SS and Police Leader East, SS General and General of the Police Krueger—or deputy

Cracow

Progress report of the grand operation on 8 May 1943. Start of operation: 1000 hours.

The entire area of the former Jewish Ghetto was searched today by assault sweep detachments for bunkers and Jews. As reported several days ago, subhumanity—bandits and terrorists—remains in bunkers, which the fires have caused to become unbearably hot. These creatures know that their choice is either to remain in hiding as long as possible or to come to the surface and try to wound or kill the men of the Waffen-SS, Police, and Wehrmacht, who keep the pressure on them.

The discovery of the bunker of the so-called inner party leadership[27] reported in yesterday's teletype message was further pursued today. We succeeded in opening the bunker of the party leadership and seizing about 60 heavily armed bandits. The deputy head of the Jewish military organization ZWZ[28] and his so-called chief of staff were caught and liquidated. About 200 Jews were sheltered in this bunker; 60 of them were apprehended and 140 destroyed due to the strong impact of smoke candles and heavy explosives laid in several places. Jews that we removed reported that countless Jews had been killed by the smoke candles. If the battle against the Jews and bandits was difficult for the first 6 days, it must now be stated that the Jews and Jewesses who bore the responsibility in those days are finally being apprehended. Every time a bunker is opened, the Jews inside offer resistance by using the weapons at their disposal, be they light machine guns, pistols, or hand grenades. Again today, a large number of Jewesses were apprehended who carried loaded pistols, their safety catches released, in their underpants.

We have statements that 3,000 to 4,000 Jews still remain in subterranean holes, sewers, and bunkers. The undersigned is determined not to terminate the grand operation until the last Jew has been destroyed.

enden, bis auch der letzte Jude vernichtet ist.

Insgesamt wurden heute aus Bunkern 1 091 Juden erfaßt, im Feuerkampf wurden etwa 280 Juden erschossen, ungezählte Juden in den
43 gesprengten Bunkern vernichtet. Die Gesamtzahl der erfaßten
Juden erhöht sich auf 49 712. Die noch nicht durch Feuer vernichteten Gebäude wurden heute angezündet und dabei festgestellt,
daß sich immer noch vereinzelte Juden irgendwie im Mauerwerk oder
in den Treppenhäusern versteckt halten.

Eigene Kräfte:

Einsatzkräfte: Deutsche Polizei   4/101
                  TN   1/6
                  Sipo   2/14
                  Pioniere (WH)   3/69
                  Waffen-SS   13/527

Absperrkräfte:	bei Tag	bei Nacht
Deutsche Polizei	1/87	1/36
Waffen-SS	-	1/300
Trawniki	160	-
poln. Polizei	1/160	1/160

Eigene Verluste: 2 Waffen-SS tot
                    2 Waffen-SS verwundet
                    1 Pionier verwundet

Ein am 7.5.43 verwundeter Angehöriger der Orpo ist heute seinen
Verletzungen erlegen.

Erbeutet wurden etwa 15 - 20 Pistolen versch. Kalibers, größere
Bestände an Pistolen und Gewehrmunition, außerdem eine Anzahl
von in den ehem. Rüstungsbetrieben selbstgefertigten Handgranaten.

Ende der Aktion: 21.30 Uhr, Fortsetzung am 9.5.43, um 10.00 Uhr.

F.d.R.:   Der SS- und Polizeiführer
                                          im Distrikt Warschau

                                       gez. Stroop

SS-Sturmbannführer.   SS-Brigadeführer
                                       u. Generalmajor der Polizei.

A total of 1,091 Jews was apprehended in the bunkers today; about 280 Jews were shot in battle; countless Jews were destroyed in 43 demolished bunkers. The total number of Jews apprehended has risen to 49,712. Buildings which had not yet been destroyed by fire were set on fire today. In the process, it was discovered that isolated Jews were still hiding somewhere within the walls or staircases.

Our forces:

Sent into action

German Police	4 officers/101 men
Technical Emergency Corps	1 officer / 6 men
Security Police	2 officers/ 14 men
Engineers (Wehrmacht)	3 officers/ 69 men
Waffen-SS	13 officers/527 men

Blockade forces

	Day	*Night*
German Police	1 officer / 87 men	1 officer / 36 men
Waffen-SS		1 officer /300 men
Trawniki	160 men	
Polish Police	1 officer /160 men	1 officer /160 men

Our losses: 2 Waffen-SS dead; 2 Waffen-SS and 1 Engineer wounded.

An Order Police wounded on 7 May 1943 today succumbed to his injuries.

15 to 20 pistols of various calibers were captured, along with considerable stores of ammunition for pistols and rifles, and a number of handmade hand grenades made in the former armament plants.

End of operations at 2130 hours. To be continued on 9 May 1943 at 1000 hours.

SS and Police Leader in the
Warsaw District

(signed) Stroop

SS Major General and Major General
of the Police

Certified copy
Jesuiter
SS Major

A b s c h r i f t !
F e r n s c h r e i b e n

Absender: Der ⚡⚡- und Polizeiführer im Distrikt Warschau

Warschau, den 9.5.43

Az.: I ab St/Gr - 16 07 - Tgb.Nr. 625/43 geh.
Betr.: Ghetto-Großaktion

An den

Höheren ⚡⚡- und Polizeiführer Ost
⚡⚡-Obergruppenführer und General der Polizei Krüger
o.V.i.A.

K r a k a u

Verlauf der Großaktion am 9.5.43, Beginn 10.00 Uhr:

Die heute durchgeführte Großaktion hatte folgendes Ergebnis:

Von den angesetzten Durchkämmungsstoßtrupps wurden 42 Bunker ermittelt. Aus diesen Bunkern wurden 1 037 Juden und Banditen lebend hervorgebracht. Im Kampf wurden erschossen 319 Banditen und Juden, außerdem ungezählte wiederum bei den Sprengungen der Bunker vernichtet. Der um den früheren Betrieb "Transavia" liegende Häuserblock wurde durch Feuer vernichtet und auf diese Weise trotz aller Durchkämmungen wiederum Juden gefangen.

Erbeutet wurden wiederum Pistolen und Handgranaten.

Eigene Kräfte:

Einsatzkräfte:	Deutsche Polizei	4/103
	Sipo	2/12
	Pioniere (WH)	3/67
	Waffen-⚡⚡	13/547

Absperrkräfte:	bei Tag	bei Nacht
Deutsche Polizei	1/87	1/36
Waffen-⚡⚡	-	1/300
Trawniki	160	-
poln. Polizei	1/160	1/160

Eigene Verluste: keine.

Die Gesamtzahl der bisher erfaßten Juden erhöht sich auf 51 313.

Außerhalb des enem. jüdischen Ghettos wurden 254 Juden und Banditen erschossen.

Ende der Aktion: 21.oo Uhr, Fortsetzung am 10.5.43, 10.oo Uhr.

F.d.R.:

[signature]

⚡⚡-Sturmbannführer.

Der ⚡⚡- und Polizeiführer
im Distrikt Warschau

gez. Stroop

⚡⚡-Brigadeführer
u. Generalmajor d.Polizei.

Copy

Teletype Message

From: SS and Police Leader in the Warsaw District

Warsaw, 9 May 1943

Ref. No.: I ab/St/Gr. 1607—*Journal No.*: 625/43 secret

Re: Grand operation in the Ghetto

To:
Higher SS and Police Leader East, SS General and General of the Police
Krueger—or deputy

Cracow

Progress report of the grand operation on 9 May 1943. Start of operation:
1000 hours.

Today's grand operation produced the following results: the assault sweep
detachments found 42 bunkers. 1,037 Jews and bandits were pulled alive
from these bunkers. 319 Jews and bandits were shot in battle, and countless
numbers were destroyed when bunkers were blown up. The housing block
surrounding the former Transavia enterprise was destroyed by fire and in
the process Jews were again caught, despite the many sweeps.

Again, pistols and hand grenades were captured.

Our forces:

Sent into action

German Police	4 officers/103 men
Security Police	2 officers/ 12 men
Engineers (Wehrmacht)	3 officers/ 67 men
Waffen-SS	13 officers/547 men

Blockade forces

	Day	Night
German Police	1 officer / 87 men	1 officer / 36 men
Waffen-SS		1 officer /300 men
Trawniki	160 men	
Polish Police	1 officer /160 men	1 officer /160 men

Our losses: none

The total number of Jews apprehended to date has risen to 51,313. 254 Jews
and bandits were shot outside the former Jewish Ghetto.

End of operations at 2100 hours. To be continued on 10 May 1943 at 1000
hours.

SS and Police Leader in the
Warsaw District

(signed) Stroop

SS Major General and Major General
of the Police

Certified copy
Jesuiter
SS Major

A b s c h r i f t .

F e r n s c h r e i b e n

Absender: Der ₴- und Polizeiführer im Distrikt Warschau

Warschau, den 10.5.1943

Az.:   I ab -St/G.- 1607 Tgb.Nr. 627/43.geh.
Betr.: Ghetto-Großaktion.

An den
Höheren ₴- und Polizeiführer Ost
₴-Obergruppenführer und General der Polizei Krüger
o.V.i.A.
K r a k a u

Verlauf der Großaktion am 10.5.43, Beginn 10.00 Uhr:

Am heutigen Tage wurde wiederum das Gebiet des ehemaligen jüd.
Wohnbezirks durch eingesetzte Durchsuchungsstoßtrupps durch-
gekämmt. Wie in den letzten Tagen wurden wider Erwarten eine
erhebliche Anzahl Juden aus den Bunkern hervorgeholt. Der von
den Juden geleistete Widerstand war heute ungeschwächt. Im Gegensatz zu den Vortagen haben sich anscheinend die noch vorhandenen und nicht vernichteten Angehörigen der jüd. Hauptkampfgruppe in die ihnen höchst erreichbaren Ruinen zurückge-
zogen, um von dort feuernd den eingesetzten Kommandos Verluste
beizubringen.

Es wurden heute insgesamt lebend 1183 Juden erfaßt. Erschossen
wurden 187 Banditen und Juden. Wiederum nicht feststellbare
Juden und Banditen wurden in den gesprengten Bunkern vernichtet. Die Gesamtzahl der bisher erfaßten Juden erhöht sich auf
52 683.

Heute um 9.00 Uhr führ ein Lkw. an einem Siel der Kanalisation
in der sog. Prosta vor. Ein Insasse dieses Lkw. brachte 2 Handgranaten zur Entzündung, die das Zeichen für die sich im Kanal
bereithaltenden Banditen war, um aus dem Siel hervorzuklettern.
Die Banditen und Juden - es befinden sich darunter auch immer
wieder poln. Banditen,-die mit Karabinern, Handfeuerwaffen und
einem lMG. bewaffnet waren - bestiegen den Lkw. und fuhren in
unbekannter Richtung davon. Der letzte Mann dieser Bande, der
Wache am Kanal hatte und den Auftrag, den Deckel der Kanalöffnung zu schließen, wurde gefangen. Von diesem stammen die vorstehend gemachten Angaben. Er erklärte, daß der größte Teil
der Bande, die in einzelne Kampfgruppen aufgeteilt war, entweder im Kampf erschossen oder sich selbst wegen der Aussichts-
losigkeit des Kampfes getötet hat. Die angesetzte Fahndung
nach dem Lkw. ist bisher ergebnislos verlaufen.

b.w.

Copy

Teletype Message

From: SS and Police Leader in the Warsaw District

Warsaw, 10 May 1943

Ref. No.: I ab/St/Gr. 1607—*Journal No.*: 627/43 secret

Re: Grand operation in the Ghetto

To:
Higher SS and Police Leader East, SS General and General of the Police Krueger—or deputy

Cracow

Progress report of the grand operation on 10 May 1943. Start of operation: 1000 hours.

Assault search detachments were again dispatched today to sweep the area of the former Jewish quarter. As on previous days, a large number of Jews were unexpectedly pulled from the bunkers. Jewish resistance continued undiminished today. Unlike on previous days, members of the main Jewish fighting group who have not been destroyed and appear to be still present retreated into the ruins which are eminently assessible to them to direct their fire and inflict casualties on our commandos.

Today, a total of 1,183 Jews was apprehended alive. 187 Jews and bandits were shot. Again, an indeterminable number of Jews and bandits were destroyed in blown-up bunkers. The total number of Jews apprehended so far has risen to 52,683.

Today at 0900 hours, a truck drove up to a manhole in the so-called Prosta. A passenger of this truck exploded 2 hand grenades, the signal for the bandits who were waiting to climb out of the manhole. The Jews and bandits—they always include Polish bandits—were armed with carbines, small arms, and 1 machine gun. They climbed into the truck and drove off in an unknown direction. The last man of this gang, who stood sentry in the sewer and was charged with closing the sewer lid, was caught. He provided this information. He explained that most members of the gang, which was subdivided into several fighting groups, had either been killed in battle or had committed suicide because of the futility of continuing the fight. The search for the truck has been fruitless so far.

Die Banditen sagten weiter aus, daß die Prosta, nachdem der Boden im ehemaligen Ghetto zu heiß wurde, der Zufluchtsort für die noch vorhandenen Juden ist. Ich habe mich aus diesem Grunde entschlossen, mit der Prosta wie mit dem Ghetto zu verfahren und dieses Zwergghetto zu vernichten.

Erbeutet wurden heute wiederum Handfeuerwaffen und Munition. Der Sicherheitspolizei gelang es am gestrigen Tage, außerhalb des Ghettos eine Werkstatt, die mit der Anfertigung von 10 - 11 000 Sprengkörpern und sonstiger Munition beschäftigt war, auszuheben.

Eigene Kräfte: Wie am Vortage.

Eigene Verluste: 3 ₭-Männer verwundet.

Auf Grund des guten Einvernehmens mit der Wehrmacht ist die Pioniergruppe weiter verstärkt worden. Desgleichen wurde auch eine größere Menge Sprengmunition zur Verfügung gestellt.

Ende der Aktion: 22.00 Uhr, Fortsetzung am 11.5.43, 9.30 Uhr.

                          Der ₭- und Polizeiführer
                            im Distrikt Warschau

                                gez. Stroop
                            ₭-Brigadeführer
                         u.Generalmajor der Polizei.

F.d.R.

₭-Sturmbannführer.

The bandits further testified that the Prosta has become the refuge for the remaining Jews because the former Ghetto has become too hot for them. For this reason, I have resolved to give the Prosta the same treatment as the Ghetto and to destroy this miniature Ghetto.

Today, small arms and ammunition again were captured. Yesterday, the Security Police succeeded in raiding a workshop outside the Ghetto which was manufacturing between 10,000 and 11,000 explosives and other ammunition.

Our forces: same as on the previous day

Our losses: 3 SS Privates wounded

The Engineer detachment was reinforced due to good relations with the Wehrmacht. On the same account, a large amount of explosives was placed at our disposal.

End of operations at 2200 hours. To be continued on 11 May 1943 at 0930 hours.

> SS and Police Leader in the
> Warsaw District
>
> (signed) Stroop
>
> SS Major General and Major General
> of the Police

Certified copy
Jesuiter
SS Major

Absender: Der ⚡⚡- und Polizeiführer im Distrikt Warschau

Warschau, den 11.5.1943

Az.: I ab -St/Gr.- 1607 Tgb.Nr. 629/43 geh.
Betr.: Ghetto-Großaktion.

An den

Höheren ⚡⚡- und Polizeiführer Ost
⚡⚡-Obergruppenführer und General d.Polizei Krüger
o.V.i.A.

K r a k a u

Verlauf der Großaktion am 11.5.43, Beginn 9.30 Uhr:

Die in der letzten Nacht angesetzten Spähtrupps meldeten erneut,
daß sich noch Juden in einigen Bunkern befinden müssen, da Juden in den zertrümmerten Straßen beobachtet wurden. Es wurden
von den Spähtrupps 12 Juden erschossen. Auf Grund dieser Meldung wurden heute erneut Durchkämmungsstoßtrupps angesetzt
mit dem Erfolg, daß insgesamt 47 Bunker festgestellt, ausgehoben und zerstört wurden. Auch heute wurden Juden, die sich in
den Mauerresten, in denen die Dächer nicht ganz zerstört waren,
festgesetzt hatten, erfaßt. Diese neuen Schlupfwinkel suchen
die Banditen und Juden auf, weil ihnen inzwischen der Aufenthalt in den Bunkern unerträglich wird. Es wurde ein Bunker
festgestellt, der etwa 12 Zimmer besaß und mit Kanalisation,
Wasser, Badeeinrichtungen für Männer und Frauen getrennt eingerichtet war. Größere Mengen an Lebensmitteln wurden erfaßt bzw.
sichergestellt, damit die Möglichkeit, sich zu reproviantieren,
immer geringer wird.

Erfaßt wurden insgesamt 931 Juden und Banditen. Erschossen
wurden 53 Banditen. In gesprengten Bunkern und bei der Vernichtung eines Häuserblocks durch Feuer kamen weitere um Leben.
Die Gesamtzahl der bisher erfaßten Juden erhöht sich auf 53 667.
Erbeutet wurden mehrere Pistolen, Handgranaten und Munition.

Eine nochmalige systematische Durchführung der Vernebelung der
Kanalisation konnte nicht erfolgen, da es an Nebelkerzen fehlt.
OFK. hat sich bereit erklärt, erneut Nebelkerzen zu besorgen.

Eigene Kräfte:

Einsatzkräfte:

Deutsche Polizei	6/126
TN	1/6
Sipo	2/14
Pioniere (WH)	4/76
Waffen-⚡⚡	12/308

b.w.

Teletype Message

From: SS and Police Leader in the Warsaw District

Warsaw, 11 May 1943

Ref. No.: I ab/St/Gr. 1607—*Journal No.*: 629/43 secret

Re: Grand operation in the Ghetto

To:
Higher SS and Police Leader East, SS General and General of the Police Krueger—or deputy

Cracow

Progress report of the grand operation on 11 May 1943. Start of operation: 0930 hours.

The reconnaissance detachments sent into action last night again reported that Jews must still be in some of the bunkers, since they were observed in the ruined streets. The reconnaissance detachments shot 12 Jews. On the basis of these reports, assault sweep detachments were once again dispatched today. The sweep netted a total of 47 bunkers, which were raided and destroyed. Today, Jews who had settled into the shells of buildings whose roofs were not totally destroyed were again apprehended. The Jews and bandits are frequenting these new hiding places because it is becoming unbearable to remain in the bunkers. One bunker containing 12 rooms equipped with plumbing, running water, and separate bath facilities for men and women was discovered. Large amounts of food were apprehended or secured to make it more difficult for Jews to resupply themselves.

A total of 931 Jews and bandits was apprehended. 53 bandits were shot. More perished when bunkers were blown up and a housing block was destroyed by fire. The total number of Jews apprehended to date has risen to 53,667. Several pistols, hand grenades, and ammunition were captured.

The sewers could not be systematically fumigated again, since there was a shortage of smoke candles. OFK[29] has agreed to procure a new supply of smoke candles.

Our forces:

Sent into action

German Police	6 officers/126 men
Technical Emergency Corps	1 officer / 6 men
Security Police	2 officers/ 14 men
Engineers (Wehrmacht)	4 officers/ 76 men
Waffen-SS	12 officers/308 men

Absperrkräfte:	bei Tag	bei Nacht
Deutsche Polizei	1/112	1/86
Waffen-ϟϟ	-	1/300
Trawniki	160	-
Poln. Polizei	1/160	1/160

Eigene Verluste: 1 ϟϟ-Mann verwundet.

Gesamtverluste: 71 Verwundete, 12 Tote.

Ende der Aktion des heutigen Unternehmens: 21.45 Uhr, Fortsetzung am 12.5.43, 9.30 Uhr.

Der ϟϟ- und Polizeiführer
im Distrikt Warschau

gez. Stroop

ϟϟ-Brigadeführer
u.Generalmajor d. Polizei

F.d.R.

ϟϟ-Sturmbannführer.

1061 PS

Blockade forces

	Day	Night
German Police	1 officer / 112 men	1 officer / 86 men
Waffen-SS		1 officer / 300 men
Trawniki	160 men	
Polish Police	1 officer / 160 men	1 officer / 160 men

Our losses: 1 SS Private wounded. Total losses to date: 71 wounded, 12 dead.

End of today's operations at 2145 hours. To be continued on 12 May 1943 at 0930 hours.

SS and Police Leader in the
Warsaw District

(signed) Stroop

SS Major General and Major General
of the Police

Certified copy
Jesuiter
SS Major

Absender: Der ⁙- und Polizeiführer im Distrikt Warschau

Warschau, den 12.5.1943

<u>Az.:</u>   I ab -St/G.- 1607 Tgb.Nr. 637/43 geh.
<u>Betr.:</u> Ghetto-Großaktion.

An den

Höheren ⁙- und Polizeiführer Ost
⁙-Obergruppenführer u. General d.Polizei Krüger
o.V.i.A.

K r a k a u

Verlauf der Großaktion am 12.5.43, Beginn: 9.30 Uhr.

Die Suche der angesetzten Durchkämmungsstoßtrupps nach weiteren
Bunkern, in denen sich Juden verborgen halten, hatte den Erfolg,
daß 30 Bunker gefunden wurden. Hieraus wurden 663 Juden hervorgeholt und 133 Juden erschossen. Die Gesamtzahl der erfaßten
Juden erhöht sich auf 54 463.

Weiter wurde heute das Zwergghetto Prosta verstärkt abgeriegelt
und durch Feuer vernichtet. Es sind wahrscheinlich eine größere
Zahl von Juden in den Flammen umgekommen. Da das Feuer vor Eintritt der Dunkelheit noch nicht niedergebrannt war, konnten ge-
naue Feststellungen in dieser Hinsicht nicht getroffen werden.
Ein Betonhaus in der Prosta, aus dem Juden hervorgeholt wurden,
wurde, um es für spätere Benutzung als Stützpunkt von Banditen
unbrauchbar zu machen, durch Sprengung vernichtet. Hierdurch
wurde die gegenüberliegende Häuserfront stark in Mitleidenschaft
gezogen. Es ist bemerkenswert, daß die Polen eine Ankündigung
sofort entsprechende Maßnahmen vor der Sprengung zur Sicherung
ihrer Fensterscheiben usw. getroffen haben.

Die nunmehr von hier abgehenden Judentransporte werden erstmalig heute nach T.II geleitet.

Eigene Kräfte:

Einsatzkräfte:	Deutsche Polizei	5/126
	TN	1/6
	Sipo	2/14
	Pioniere (WH)	4/74
	Waffen-⁙	12/508

Absperrkräfte:	bei Tag	bei Nacht
Deutsche Polizei	1/112	1/86
Waffen-⁙	-	1/300
Trawniki	160	-
poln. Polizei	1/160	1/160

b.w.

Copy

Teletype Message

From: SS and Police Leader in the Warsaw District

Warsaw, 12 May 1943

Ref. No.: I ab/St/Gr. 1607—*Journal No.*: 637/43 secret

Re: Grand operation in the Ghetto

To:

Higher SS and Police Leader East, SS General and General of the Police Krueger—or deputy

Cracow

Progress report of the grand operation on 12 May 1943. Start of operation: 0930 hours.

The assault sweep detachments' search for further bunkers where Jews are hiding resulted in the discovery of 30 bunkers. 663 Jews were pulled from them and 133 were shot. The total number of Jews apprehended has risen to 54,463.

Further, the miniature Ghetto Prosta was more completely sealed off today and destroyed by fire. A large number of Jews probably perished in the flames. Accurate information in this regard could not be obtained because the fire was still blazing when darkness fell. A concrete house in the Prosta from which Jews had been removed was blown up to render it useless as a future base for the bandits. The front of the house directly across the street was heavily damaged as a result. It is noteworthy that lacking any announcement from us, the Poles nonetheless immediately took appropriate measures to protect their windowpanes, etc., before the explosion.

Starting today, the transports of Jews leaving from here will be sent to T II.

Our forces:

Sent into action

German Police	5 officers/126 men
Technical Emergency Corps	1 officer / 6 men
Security Police	2 officers/ 14 men
Engineers	4 officers/ 74 men
Waffen-SS	12 officers/508 men

Blockade forces

	Day	Night
German Police	1 officer /112 men	1 officer / 86 men
Waffen-SS		1 officer /300 men
Trawniki	160 men	
Polish Police	1 officer /160 men	1 officer /160 men

Eigene Verluste: 1 Mann Waffen-SS verwundet.

Ende des heutigen Unternehmens: 21.00 Uhr. Fortsetzung am 13.5.43 um 10.00 Uhr.

Der SS- und Polizeiführer
im Distrikt Warschau

gez. Stroop

SS-Brigadeführer
und Generalmajor d.Polizei

F.d.R.

SS-Sturmbannführer.

Our losses: 1 SS Private wounded

End of today's undertaking at 2100 hours. To be continued on 13 May 1943 at 1000 hours.

> SS and Police Leader in the
> Warsaw District
>
> (signed) Stroop
>
> SS Major General and Major General
> of the Police

Certified copy
Jesuiter
SS Major

F e r n s c h r e i b e n

Absender: Der ⚡- und Polizeiführer im Distrikt Warschau

Warschau, den 13. Mai 1943

<u>Az.:</u> I ab -St/Gr.- 1607 Tgb.Nr. 641/43 geh.
<u>Betr.:</u>Ghetto-Großaktion.

An den
Höheren ⚡- und Polizeiführer Ost
⚡-Obergruppenführer u. General d. Polizei Krüger
o.V.i.A.
K r a k a u

Verlauf der Großaktion am 13.5.43, Beginn: 10.00 Uhr:

Bei der heutigen Durchkämmung des großen und kleinen Ghettos
(Prosta) wurden 234 Juden gestellt. Im Kampf wurden 155 Juden
erschossen. Es zeigte sich am heutigen Tage, daß die nunmehr
gefangenen Juden und Banditen den sogen. Kampfgruppen angehören.
Es sind durchweg junge Burschen und Weiber im Alter von 18 - 25
Jahren. Bei der Aushebung eines Bunkers entspann sich ein regel-
rechtes Feuergefecht, bei dem die Juden nicht nur aus Pistolen
08 und poln. Vis-Pistolen schossen, sondern auch poln. Eierhandgranaten gegen die Männer der Waffen-⚡ warfen. Nachdem ein Teil
der Bunkerbesatzung ausgehoben war und diese durchsucht werden
sollte, griff eins der Weiber wie schon so oft blitzschnell
unter ihren Rock und holte aus ihrem Schlüpfer eine Eierhand-
granate hervor, die sie abzog und unter die sie durchsuchenden
Männer warf, dabei blitzschnell selbst in Deckung sprang. Nur
der Geistesgegenwart der Männer ist es zu verdanken, daß kein
Ausfall eintrat.

Die wenigen sich noch im Ghetto aufhaltenden Juden und Verbrecher
benützen seit 2 Tagen die noch in Ruinen sich bietenden Schlupfwinkel, um nachts in die ihnen bekannten Bunker zurückzukehren,
dort zu essen und sich wieder für den nächsten Tag zu verprovi-
antieren. Eine Aussage über weiter ihnen bekannte Bunker von den
gefangenen Juden herauszuholen, ist neuerdings unmöglich. Der
Rest der Besatzung, bei dem das Feuergefecht stattfand, wurde
durch stärkste Sprengladungen vernichtet. Aus einem Wehrmachts-
betrieb wurden heute 327 Juden erfaßt. Die jetzt erfaßten Juden
werden nur nach T.II geleitet.

Die Gesamtzahl der erfaßten Juden erhöht sich auf 55 179.

Eigene Kräfte:
<u>Einsatzkräfte:</u>

Deutsche Polizei	4/182
TN	1/6
Sipo	2/14
Pioniere (WH)	4/74
Waffen-⚡	12/517

b.w.

Teletype Message

From: SS and Police Leader in the Warsaw District

Warsaw, 13 May 1943

Ref. No.: I ab/St/Gr. 1607—*Journal No.*: 641/43 secret

Re: Grand operation in the Ghetto

To:
Higher SS and Police Leader East, SS General and General of the Police Krueger—or deputy

Cracow

Progress report of the grand operation on 13 May 1943. Start of operation: 1000 hours.

During today's sweep of the large and small Ghetto (Prosta), 234 Jews were arrested. 155 Jews were shot in battle. Today, it became clear that the Jews and bandits now being caught belong to the so-called fighting groups. All of them are young men and women between 18 and 25 years of age. A real skirmish developed while one bunker was being cleared. The Jews not only fired .08-caliber pistols and Polish Vis-pistols but also threw Polish oval hand grenades at the men of the Waffen-SS. As soon as some of the inhabitants had been cleared from the bunker and were about to be searched, one of the females, as so often happens, put her hand under her skirt and, quick as lightning, pulled an oval hand grenade from her underpants, pulled the safety pin, threw the grenade into the group of men conducting the search, and herself jumped for cover quick as lightning. No casualties resulted, thanks to the presence of mind shown by the men.

During the last two days, the few Jews and criminals remaining in the Ghetto made use of hideouts still found among the ruins and returned at night to bunkers known to them to eat and get provisions for the next day. It has recently become impossible to extract information about other bunkers from the captured Jews. The remaining occupants of the bunker involved in the skirmish were destroyed with heavy explosives. 327 Jews were apprehended today in a Wehrmacht enterprise. The Jews that are apprehended now are all sent to T II. The total number of Jews apprehended has risen to 55,179.

Our forces:

Sent into action

German Police	4 officers/182 men
Technical Emergency Corps	1 officer / 6 men
Security Police	2 officers/ 14 men
Engineers	4 officers/ 74 men
Waffen-SS	12 officers/517 men

Absperrkräfte:	bei Tag	bei Nacht
Deutsche Polizei	2/137	1/87
Waffen-ϟϟ	-	1/300
Trawniki	270	-
Poln. Polizei	1/160	1/160

Eigene Verluste: 2 Waffen-ϟϟ tot
3 Waffen-ϟϟ verwundet
1 Polizeiangeh. verwundet.

Dei beiden gefallenen Männer der Waffen-ϟϟ sind während des Flieger-
angriffes im Ghetto ums Leben gekommen.

33 Bunker sind erfaßt und vernichtet. Beute: 6 Pistolen, 2 Handgranaten und Sprengkörper.

Ende des heutigen Unternehmens: 21.00 Uhr, Fortsetzung am 14.5.43,
um 10.00 Uhr.

Ich beabsichtige, die Großaktion an 16.5.43 zu beenden und die
weiteren durchzuführenden Maßnahmen dem Polizeibataillon III/23 zu
übertragen. Ein ausführlicher Bericht mit Bildanhang werde ich,
falls kein anderer Befehl folgt, bei der ϟϟ- und Polizeiführertagung
vorlegen.

Der ϟϟ- und Polizeiführer
im Distrikt Warschau

gez. Stroop

ϟϟ-Brigadeführer
u. Generalmajor d. Polizei.

F.d.R.

ϟϟ-Sturmbannführer.

Blockade forces

	Day	Night
German Police	2 officers/137 men	1 officer / 87 men
Waffen-SS		1 officer /300 men
Trawniki	270 men	
Polish Police	1 officer /160 men	1 officer /160 men

Our losses: 2 Waffen-SS dead; 3 Waffen-SS and 1 Police wounded.

Both Waffen-SS men lost their lives in an air-raid attack in the Ghetto.[30]

33 bunkers were taken and destroyed. Booty: 6 pistols, 2 hand grenades, and explosives.

End of today's undertaking at 2100 hours. To be continued on 14 May 1943 at 1000 hours.

I intend to conclude the grand operation on 16 May 1943 and to transfer the implementation of further measures to Police Battalion III/23. I will submit a detailed report with a pictorial appendix to the conference of SS and Police Leaders, pending no other orders.

SS and Police Leader in the
Warsaw District

(signed) Stroop

SS Major General and Major General
of the Police

Certified copy
Jesuiter
SS Major

F e r n s c h r e i b e n

Absender: Der ₰- und Polizeiführer im Distrikt Warschau ·

Warschau, den 14. Mai 1943

Az.:   I ab -St/Gr.- 1607 Tgb.Nr. 646/43 geh.
Betr.: Gehtto-Großaktion.

An den
Höheren ₰- und Polizeiführer Ost
₰-Obergruppenführer u. General der Pol. Krüger
o.V.i.A.
K r a k a u

Verlauf der Großaktion am 14.5.43, Beginn 10.00 Uhr:

Die eingeteilten Durchkämmungsstoßtrupps nahmen ihre Tätigkeit
in den ihnen zugewiesenen Abschnitten wieder auf mit dem Auftrag,
weitere Wohnbunker zu öffnen und die Juden zu erfassen. Auf diese
Weise wurde heute wiederum eine größere Zahl von Banditen und
Juden erfaßt. Insbes. wurden einige in der Nacht entdeckte Spu-
ren weiter mit gutem Ergebnis verfolgt. Die Nachtstoßtrupps hatten verschiedentlich Zusammenstöße mit bewaffneten Banditen.
Diese schossen mit MG. und Handfeuerwaffen. Hierdurch traten
auf unsere Seite vier Ausfälle ein, davon 3 Waffen-₰ und 1
Ordnungspolizei. ·Es wurde wiederholt aus dem arischen Teil auf
die äußere Absperrung geschossen. Von der Postenkette wurde
rücksichtslos das Feuer erwidert. Bei den Zusammenstößen wurden
etwa 30 Banditen erschossen und 9 Juden und Banditen, die einer
bewaffneten Bande angehörten, gefangen. Ein Bunker wurde in der
Nacht ausgehoben, die Juden gefangen und einige Pistolen, darunter 12 mit Kaliber, erbeutet. In einem Bunker, der mit etwa
100 Personen besetzt war, konnten 2 Gewehre, 16 Pistolen, Hand-
und Brandgranaten erbeutet werden. Von den sich zur Wehr setzenden Banditen trugen wiederum verschiedene deutsche Wehrmachts-
uniform und deutsche Stahlhelme und Knobelbecher. Außer den
Karabinern wurden 60 Schuß deutsche Gewehrmunition eingebracht.
1 Stoßtrupp hatte ein Feuergefecht mit einer 10 - 14köpfigen
Bande auf den Dächern eines Häuserblocks am Rande des Ghettos
(arischer Teil). Die Banditen wurden ohne eigene Verluste vernichtet.

Die gefangenen Banditen sagen wiederholt aus, daß noch nicht
alle Personen im Ghetto erfaßt seien. Sie rechnen stark damit,
daß die Aktion bald beendet wird, um dann wieder im Ghetto
weiterleben zu können. Verschiedene Banditen ließen sich dahin-
gehend aus, daß sie den Führer der Aktion, "General" wie sie
ihn nennen, längst hätten umlegen können, dieses aber befehls-
gemäß nicht tun würden, um die gegen die Juden ergriffenen
Maßnahmen dadurch nicht noch weiter zu verschärfen.

                                                    b.w.

Copy

Teletype Message

From: SS and Police Leader in the Warsaw District

Warsaw, 14 May 1943

Ref. No.: I ab/St/Gr. 1607—*Journal No.*: 646/43 secret

Re: Grand operation in the Ghetto

To:
Higher SS and Police Leader East, SS General and General of the Police
Krueger—or deputy

Cracow

Progress report of the grand operation on 14 May 1943. Start of operation:
1000 hours.

The assault sweep detachments went into action in their assigned areas with
orders to open more residential bunkers and apprehend the Jews. In this way,
a large number of Jews and bandits were apprehended again today. Above
all, trails discovered during the night were followed with good results. The
night assault detachments clashed several times with armed bandits, who fired
small arms and a machine gun. Our side suffered 4 casualties—3 Waffen-SS
and 1 Order Police. Shots were repeatedly fired from the Aryan section
against the surrounding barricade. The line of sentries returned relentless
fire. About 30 bandits were shot in the skirmishes, and 9 Jews and bandits
belonging to an armed gang were captured. One bunker was cleared during
the night, the Jews captured, and some pistols, including 12mm-caliber
weapons, seized. 2 rifles, 16 pistols, hand grenades, and incendiary grenades
were captured in another bunker, occupied by about 100 people. Some of
the bandits who resisted again wore various German Army uniforms, German
steel helmets, and boots. In addition to carbines, 60 rounds of German rifle
ammunition were taken. One assault detachment got into a skirmish with
a 10- to 14-member gang on the roofs of a housing block at the edge of the
Ghetto (Aryan part). The bandits were exterminated, with no losses on our
side.

The captured bandits repeatedly testify that not all persons in the Ghetto
have been apprehended. They confidently expect that the operation will soon
be over and that they will then be able to continue living in the Ghetto.
Several bandits expressed themselves along the line that they could have killed
the leader of the operation, the "General" as they call him, all along but re-
frained from violating orders in order not to risk an intensification of anti-
Jewish measures.

Heute wurden weiter einige Betonhäuser, in denen sich immer wieder die Banditen festsetzen, von den Pionieren gesprengt.

Um die Banditen aus der Kanalisation an die Oberfläche zu bringen, wurden um 15.00 Uhr 183 Kanaleinsteiglöcher geöffnet und in diese zu einer festgelegten X-Zeit Nebelkerzen herabgelassen mit dem Erfolg, daß die Banditen, vor dem angeblichen Gas flüchtend, im Zentrum des ehem. jüdischen Wohnbezirks zusammenliefen und aus den dort befindlichen Kanalöffnungen herausgeholt werden konnten.

Wegen der Beendigung der Aktion werde ich mich nach Verlauf des morgigen Tages entscheiden.

Heute nachmittag wohnte SS-Gruppenführer und Generalleutnant der Waffen-SS v. H e r f f dem angesetzten Unternehmen bei.

Eigene Kräfte:

Einsatzkräfte:

Deutsche Polizei	4/184
TN	1/6
Sicherheitspolizei	2/16
Pioniere (WH)	4/73
Waffen-SS	12/510

Absperrkräfte:	bei Tag	bei Nacht
Deutsche Polizei	2/138	1/87
Waffen-SS	-	1/300
Trawniki	-/270	-
poln. Polizei	1/160	1/160.

Eigene Verluste: 5 Verwundete, davon 4 Waffen-SS, 1 Ordnungspolizei.

Insgesamt wurden heute 398 Juden erfaßt, ausserdem im Kampf 154 Juden und Banditen erschossen. Die Gesamtzahl der erfaßten Juden erhöht sich dadurch auf 55 731.

Beute: Gewehre, Pistolen und Munition. Ausserdem eine Anzahl Brandflaschen (Molotow-Cocktails).

Ende der Aktion: 21.15 Uhr. Fortsetzung am 15.5.43, 9.00 Uhr.

Der SS- und Polizeiführer
im Distrikt Warschau

gez. Stroop
SS-Brigadeführer
und Generalmajor d. Polizei.

F.d.R.

SS-Sturmbannführer.

1061 PS
23

Today, the Engineers again blew up several concrete houses where bandits continued to find refuge.

To drive the bandits out of the sewer network, 183 manholes were opened at 1500 hours and smoke candles were lowered at a predetermined hour to force the bandits to the surface. The bandits fled from what they thought was gas into the center of the former Jewish quarter, where they were pulled from the manholes.

I will decide about the termination of the operation after tomorrow's engagement.

SS Lieutenant-General and Lieutenant-General of the Waffen-SS von Herff was in attendance during this afternoon's undertaking.[31]

Our forces:

Sent into action

German Police	4 officers/184 men
Technical Emergency Corps	1 officer / 6 men
Security Police	2 officers/ 16 men
Engineers	4 officers/ 73 men
Waffen-SS	12 officers/510 men

Blockade forces

	Day	Night
German Police	2 officers/138 men	1 officer / 87 men
Waffen-SS		1 officer /300 men
Trawniki	270 men	
Polish Police	1 officer /160 men	1 officer /160 men

Our losses: 5 wounded, including 4 Waffen-SS and 1 Order Police

A total of 398 Jews was apprehended today, another 154 Jews and bandits shot in battle. Thus, the total number of Jews apprehended has risen to 55,731.

Booty: rifles, pistols, and ammunition; also, a number of incendiary bottles (Molotov cocktails)

End of operations at 2115 hours. To be continued on 15 May 1943 at 0900 hours.

> SS and Police Leader in the
> Warsaw District
>
> (signed) Stroop
>
> SS Major General and Major General
> of the Police

Certified copy
Jesuiter
SS Major

F e r n s c h r e i b e n

Absender: Der ⚡⚡- und Polizeiführer im Distrikt Warschau

Warschau, den 15. Mai 1943

Az.: I ab -St/Gr.- 16o7 Tgb.Nr. 648/43 geh.

Betr.: Ghetto-Großaktion.

An den

Höheren ⚡⚡- und Polizeiführer Ost
⚡⚡-Obergruppenführer und General d. Polizei Krüger
o.V.i.A.

K r a k a u

Verlauf der Großaktion am 15.5.43, Beginn 9.00 Uhr:

Die in der letzten Nacht das Ghetto durchstreifenden Spähtrupps
haben gemeldet, daß nur ganz vereinzelt Juden angetroffen wurden.
Es konnten im Gegensatz zu den vergangenen Nächten nur 6 oder
7 Juden erschossen werden. Die heute angesetzten Durchsuchungsstoßtrupps hatten ebenfalls nur einen kleinen Erfolg. Es wurden
29 neue Bunker ermittelt, die aber schon teilweise keine Insassen
mehr hatten. Insgesamt wurden heute 87 Juden erfaßt und außerdem im Kampf 67 Banditen und Juden erschossen. Bei einem sich
in der Mittagszeit entwickelnden Feuergefecht, bei dem die Banditen wiederum mit Molotow-Cocktails, Pistolen und selbstgefertigten Handgranaten sich zur Wehr setzten, wurde nach der Vernichtung der Bande ein Angehöriger der Ordnungspolizei durch
Durchschuß der rechten Hüfte verwundet.

Durch ein Sonderkommando wurde der letzte noch vorhandene unver-
sehrte Gebäudekomplex des Ghettos nochmals durchsucht und anschließend vernichtet. Am Abend wurden auf dem jüdischen Friedhof die Kapelle, Leichenhalle und sämtliche Nebengebäude gesprengt bzw. durch Feuer vernichtet. Die Gesamtzahl der erfaßten
Juden erhöht sich auf 55.885.

Eigene Kräfte:

Einsatzkräfte:	Deutsche Polizei	4/184
	TN	1/6
	Sipo	2/16
	Pioniere (WH)	4/73
	Waffen-⚡⚡	12/510

Absperrkräfte:	bei Tag	bei Nacht
Deutsche Pol.	2/138	1/87
Waffen-⚡⚡	-	1/300
Trawniki	270	-
Poln. Polizei	1/160	1/160.

b.w.

Teletype Message

From: SS and Police Leader in the Warsaw District

Warsaw, 15 May 1943

Ref. No.: I ab/St/Gr. 1607—*Journal No.*: 648/43 secret

Re: Grand operation in the Ghetto

To:

Higher SS and Police Leader East, SS General and General of the Police Krueger—or deputy

Cracow

Progress report of the grand operation on 15 May 1943. Start of operation: 0900 hours.

The reconnaissance detachments patrolling the Ghetto last night reported only sporadic encounters with Jews. In contrast to preceding nights, only 6 to 7 Jews were shot. The assault sweep detachments dispatched today also had only minor success. 29 new bunkers were discovered, but some of them no longer had occupants. Altogether, 87 Jews were apprehended today and an additional 67 Jews and bandits shot in battle. In a skirmish that developed around noon, the bandits again resisted, using Molotov cocktails, pistols, and homemade hand grenades. The gang was destroyed, but subsequently 1 member of the Order Police was shot through the right hip.

A special commando unit once more searched the last building complex, which had been left standing intact in the Ghetto, and subsequently destroyed it. In the evening, the chapel, mortuary, and all other buildings at the Jewish cemetery were blown up or destroyed by fire.

The total number of Jews apprehended has risen to 55,885.

Our forces:

Sent into action

German Police	4 officers/184 men
Technical Emergency Corps	1 officer / 6 men
Security Police	2 officers/ 16 men
Engineers (Wehrmacht)	4 officers/ 73 men
Waffen-SS	12 officers/510 men

Blockade forces

	Day	Night
German Police	2 officers/138 men	1 officer / 87 men
Waffen-SS		1 officer /300 men
Trawniki	270 men	
Polish Police	1 officer /160 men	1 officer /160 men

Eigene Verluste: 1 Orpo verwundet.

Erbeutet wurden: 4 Pistolen größeren Kalibers, 1 Höllenmaschine
                  mit Zündkabel, 10 kg Sprengstoff sowie eine
                  größere Menge Munition.

Ende der Aktion: 21.30 Uhr, Fortsetzung am 16.5.43, 10.00 Uhr.

Ich werde die Großaktion am 16.5.43, gegen Abend, mit der heute
nicht geglückten Sprengung der Synagoge beenden und das Polizei-
bataillon III/23 mit der Fortsetzung bzw. Beendung der noch durchzuführenden Maßnahmen beauftragen.

                              Der ⚡⚡- und Polizeiführer
                                im Distrikt Warschau

                                  gez. Stroop

                              ⚡⚡-Brigadeführer
                           und Generalmajor d⚡ Polizei.

F.d.R.

⚡⚡-Sturmbannführer.

Our losses: 1 Order Police wounded

Booty captured: 4 pistols of large calibers, 1 time bomb with fuse, 10 kilograms of explosives, and a large quantity of ammunition

End of operations at 2130 hours. To be continued on 16 May 1943 at 1000 hours.

I will terminate the grand operation on 16 May 1943 at dusk, blowing up the synagogue, which we failed to accomplish today. I will commission Police Battalion III/23 to continue or complete any necessary measures.

SS and Police Leader in the
Warsaw District

(signed) Stroop

SS Major General and Major General
of the Police

Certified copy
Jesuiter
SS Major

A b s c h r i f t.

F e r n s c h r e i b e n

Absender: Der ϟϟ- und Polizeiführer im Distrikt Warschau

Warschau, den   16. Mai 1943

Az.: I ab - St/Gr. - 1607 Tgb.Nr. 652/43 geh.

Betr.:Ghetto-Großaktion.

An den
Höheren ϟϟ- und Polizeiführer Ost
ϟϟ-Obergruppenführer und Genral d. Polizei Krüger
o.V.i.A.
K r a k a u

Verlauf der Großaktion am 16.5.43, Beginn 10.00 Uhr:

Es wurden 180 Juden, Banditen und Untermenschen vernichtet.
Das ehemalige jüdische Wohnviertel Warschau besteht nicht
mehr. Mit der Sprengung der Warschauer Synagoge wurde die
Großaktion um 20.15 Uhr beendet.

Die für die errichteten Sperrgebiete weiter zu treffenden Maßnahmen sind dem Kommandeur des Pol.-Batl. III/23 nach eingehen-
der Einweisung übertragen.

Gesamtzahl der erfaßten und nachweislich vernichteten Juden be-
trägt insgesamt 56 065.

Keine eigenen Verluste.

Schlußbericht lege ich am 18.5.43 bei der ϟϟ- und Polizeiführertagung vor.

Der ϟϟ- und Polizeiführer
im Distrikt Warschau

gez. Stroop
ϟϟ-Brigadeführer
u. Generalmajor d. Polizei

F.d.R.

ϟϟ-Sturmbannführer.

Copy

Teletype Message

From: SS and Police Leader in the Warsaw District

Warsaw, 16 May 1943

Ref. No.: I ab/St/Gr. 1607—*Journal No.*: 652/43 secret

Re: Grand operation in the Ghetto

To:
Higher SS and Police Leader East, SS General and General of the Police Krueger—or deputy

Cracow

Progress report of the grand operation on 16 May 1943. Start of operation: 1000 hours.

180 Jews, bandits, and subhumans were destroyed. The Jewish quarter of Warsaw is no more! The grand operation terminated at 2015 hours when the Warsaw synagogue was blown up.

To the Commander of Police Battalion III/23, who received a thorough induction, were transferred all necessary measures to be taken concerning the restricted areas that have been established.

The total number of Jews apprehended and destroyed, according to record, is 56,065.

We had no losses.

I will submit the final report to the conference of SS and Police Leaders on 18 May 1943.

> SS and Police Leader in the
> Warsaw District
>
> (signed) Stroop
>
> SS Major General and Major General
> of the Police

Certified copy
Jesuiter
SS Major

Absender: Der ⚡- und Polizeiführer im Distrikt Warschau

Warschau, den 24. Mai 1943.

Az.: I ab -St/Gr- 16 07 - Tgb.Nr. 663/43 geh.
Betr.: Ghetto-Großaktion
Bezug: Dort. FS Nr. 946 v. 21.5.43.

An den
Höheren ⚡- und Polizeiführer Ost
⚡-Obergruppenführer und General d. Polizei
K r ü g e r - o.V.i.A.

K r a k a u

Obenbezeichnetes Fernschreiben beantworte ich wie folgt:

Zu Ziff. 1

Von den 56 065 insgesamt erfaßten Juden sind ca. 7 000 im Zuge
der Großaktion im ehem. jüd. Wohnbezirk selbst vernichtet. Durch
Transport nach T. II wurden 6 929 Juden vernichtet, so daß
insges. 13 929 Juden vernichtet wurden. Über die Zahl 56 065
hinaus sind schätzungsweise 5 - 6 000 Juden bei Sprengungen und
durch Feuer vernichtet worden.

Zu Ziff. 2

Es wurden 631 Bunker vernichtet.

Zu Ziff. 3 (Beute)

7 poln. Gewehre, 1 russ. Gewehr, 1 deutsches Gewehr,
59 Pistolen versch. Kaliber's,
mehrere 100 Handgranaten, darunter polnische und selbstgefertigte,
einige 100 Brandflaschen,
selbstgefertigte Sprengkörper,
Höllenmaschinen mit Zündkabel.

Große Mengen Sprengstoffe, Munition für Waffen aller Kaliber,
darunter auch MG-Munition.

Bei der Beute an Waffen ist zu berücksichtigen, daß die Waffen
selbst in den meisten Fällen nicht erfaßt werden konnten, weil
sie von den Banditen und Juden in nicht festzustellende oder auf-
findbare Verstecke und Löcher vor Gefangennahme weggeworfen wurden. Die Erfassung war auch wegen der Vernebelung der Bunker
durch unsere Männer unmöglich. Da die Sprengung der Bunker sofort
vorgenommen werden mußte, kam eine spätere Erfassung nicht in Be-
tracht.

Die erbeuteten Handgranaten, die Sprengmunition und die Brandflaschen fanden bei Bekämpfung der Banditen durch uns sofort wieder
Verwendung.

b.w.

Teletype Message

From: SS and Police Leader in the Warsaw District

Warsaw, 24 May 1943

Ref. No.: I ab/St/Gr. 1607—*Journal No.*: 663/43 secret

Re: Grand operation in the Ghetto

Ref: Your teletype message No. 946 on 21 May 1943

To:

Higher SS and Police Leader East, SS General and General of the Police Krueger—or deputy

Cracow

I reply to the above-referenced message as follows:

Re: Number 1

Of the total 56,065 Jews apprehended, about 7,000 were destroyed directly in the course of the grand operation in the former Jewish quarter. 6,929 Jews were destroyed via transport to T II, making the total number of Jews destroyed 13,929. In addition to this figure of 56,065, an estimated 5,000 to 6,000 Jews were destroyed in explosions or fires.

Re: Number 2

631 bunkers were destroyed.

Re: Number 3

7 Polish rifles, 1 USSR rifle, 1 German rifle, 59 pistols of various calibers

Several hundred hand grenades, including Polish and homemade ones

A few hundred incendiary bottles

Homemade explosives

Time bombs with fuses

Large quantities of explosives, ammunition for weapons of all calibers, including machine-gun ammunition

Regarding the capture of arms, it must be taken into account that in most cases, arms could not be taken because the Jews and bandits, before their own capture, would throw them into hideouts and holes that could not be located or found. The fumigation of the bunkers also made it impossible for our men to take arms. Since we had to blow up the bunkers immediately, it was not feasible to take arms later on.

The hand grenades, explosives, and incendiary bottles captured by us were immediately put to use against the bandits.

Weiter wurden erbeutet:

1 240 alte Waffenröcke (z.T. mit Ordensbändern – EK und Ostmedaille versehen-)
600 alte Hosen
Ausrüstungsstücke und deutsche Stahlhelme
108 Pferde, davon 4 noch im ehem. Ghetto (Leichenwagen).

Bis zum 23.5.43 wurden gezählt:

4,4 Mill. Zloty, außerdem ungezählt etwa 5 – 6 Mill. Zloty,
eine große Menge Devisen, unter anderem 14 300 Dollar Papier-
scheine und 9 200 Golddollar, außerdem Schmucksachen (Ringe,
Ketten, Uhren usw.) in großen Mengen.

Zu Ziff. 4

Bis auf 8 Gebäude (Polizeiunterkunft, Krankenhaus und vorgesehene Unterkunft für Werkschutz) ist das ehem. Ghetto voll-
ständig zerstört. Soweit nicht Sprengungen durchgeführt wurden, stehen nur noch die Brandmauern. Aus den Ruinen sind
aber noch Steine und Schrott in unübersehbarer Menge zu ver-
werten.

Der ﬡ- und Polizeiführer
im Distrikt Warschau

gez. Stroop

ﬡ-Brigadeführer
und Generalmajor d. Polizei.

F.d.R.:

ﬡ-Sturmbannführer.

Further captured were:
1,240 used uniform jackets (some with medal ribbons—Iron Cross and East Medal)
600 pairs of used trousers
Equipment items and German steel helmets
108 horses, 4 still remaining in the former Ghetto (hearse)

Counted as of 23 May 1943:
4.4 million zloty; further uncounted, about 4 to 5 million zloty;[32] a large amount of foreign currency, including $14,300 in paper bills and 9,200 gold dollars; also large amounts of jewelry (rings, necklaces, watches, etc.)

Re: Number 4
The former Ghetto has been completely destroyed, except for 8 buildings (police barracks, hospital, and accommodations designated for plant security). Only fire walls are left standing where no explosives were set. However, the ruins would yield enormous quantities of stone and scrap material for further utilization.

SS and Police Leader in the
Warsaw District

(signed) Stroop

SS Major General and Major General
of the Police

Certified copy
Jesuiter
SS Major

Bildbericht.

PICTORIAL
REPORT

~ Das Gebäude des ehemaligen Judenrats. ~

The building of the former Jewish Council

— Heraus aus den Betrieben! —

Vacate the plants!

Die Räumung eines Betriebes wird besprochen.

Discussing the evacuation of an enterprise

The Jewish department heads of the armament firm Brauer

Firma Brauer.

The Brauer firm

~ Mit Gewalt aus Bunkern hervorgeholt. ~

Pulled from the bunkers by force

~ Nach dem Umschlagplatz. ~

To the *Umschlagplatz*

~ Durchsuchung und Verhör. ~

Search and interrogation

Jüdische Rabiner.

Jewish rabbis[33]

~ Jüdische Rabiner ~

Jewish rabbis

~ Abschaum der Menschheit. ~

Dregs of humanity

~ Ein Stoßtrupp. ~

An assault detachment

Mit Gewalt aus Bunkern hervorgeholt.

Pulled from the bunkers by force

~ Diese Banditen verteidigten sich mit der Waffe. ~

These bandits offered armed resistance

~ Soeben aus einem Bunker hervorgeholt. ~

Just pulled from a bunker

~ Banditen. ~

Bandits

K. 1037

~ *Im Kampfe vernichtete Banditen.* ~

Bandits destroyed in battle

— Ein Bunker wird geöffnet. —

A bunker being opened

~ Jüdische Verräter. ~

Jewish traitors

— Ausräucherung der Juden u. Banditen. —

Smoking out the Jews and bandits

— Zür Flucht und zum Absprung vorbereiteter querspur Platz. —

A spot that had been readied for escape and jumping

~ Vernichtung eines Häuserblocks. ~

Destruction of a housing block

He-halutz women captured with weapons

~ Ein Häuserblock wird vernichtet. ~

A housing block being destroyed

~ Abtransport von Juden. ~

Transporting Jews onward

~ Bilder aus dem Wohnbunkern. ~

Pictures of so-called residential bunkers

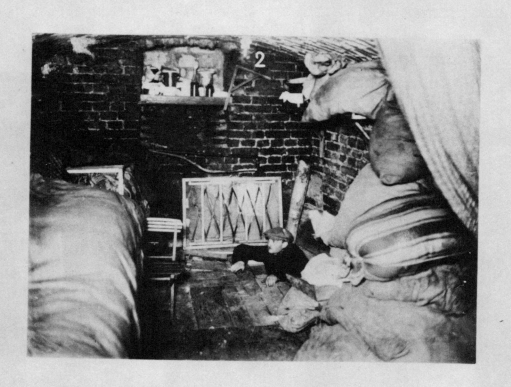

F. 626/11.

Before the search

~ Vor der Durchsuchung ~

Securing a street

~ Sicherung einer Straße ~

They were also found in underground bunkers.

~ Auch in Bunkern unter der Erde wurden sie gefunden. ~

In combat against a resistance pocket

~ Bekämpfung eines Widerstandsnestes. ~

In combat against a resistance pocket

~ *Bekämpfung eines Widerstandnestes.* ~

Bandits jump to escape arrest

~ *Die Banditen entziehen sich der Festnahme durch Absprung.* ~

~ Abspringen Banditen. ~

Bandits who jumped

~ Der Funkwagen des Befehlshabers. ~

Radio car of the command post

Askaris assigned to the operation[34]

— Askaris, die mit eingesetzt waren. —

The leader of the grand operation

— Der Führer der Großaktion. —

~ So sieht es in einem jüdischen Wohnbezirk nach der Vernichtung aus. ~

Views of the former Jewish quarter after its destruction

46

47

48

Archiwum
Głównej Komisji Badania
Zbrodni Niem. w Polsce
Dok. N. 55/2027 Nr. 4529

NOTES

1. SS and police ranks have been translated into U. S. Army equivalents on the basis of a table reproduced in Helmut Krausnick et al., *Anatomy of the SS State*, trans. Richard Barry, Marian Jackson, and Dorothy Lang (London: Collins, 1968).

2. The *Ordnungspolizei* (Order Police) consisted of the *Schutzpolizei* (Protective Police), or regular urban police, and the *Gendarmerie*, or rural police. The *Sicherheitspolizei*, or *Sipo* (Security Police), encompassed the *Kriminalpolizei*, or *Kripo* (Criminal Police), and the newly formed *Geheime Staatspolizei*, or *Gestapo* (Secret State Police). Heinrich Himmler, in his dual role as Reich Leader SS and Chief of the German Police, had jurisdiction over both SS and police forces. Most senior police officers also held SS ranks.

3. Trawniki men were Ukrainian and Baltic SS units trained at the Trawniki Labor Camp, a satellite of the Lublin Concentration Camp.

4. The *Aeltestenrat* (Council of Elders) is another name for the *Judenrat* (Jewish Council). The decree of 28 November 1939 issued by the General Government required every Jewish community to establish Jewish Councils.

5. This was part of *Aktion Reinhard*, or the "Great Liquidation." 310,322 Jews were deported to Treblinka, and 5,961 Jews were killed inside the Warsaw Ghetto. This left an estimated 60,000 to 70,000 Jews in Warsaw. Good contemporary accounts can be found in Bernard Goldstein, *Five Years in the Warsaw Ghetto*, trans. Leonard Shatzkin (Garden City, N.Y.: Doubleday and Co., 1961); Gerald Reitlinger, *The Final Solution: The Attempt to Exterminate the Jews of Europe, 1939–1945* (New York: A. S. Barnes & Co., 1961), pp. 244–71; and World Jewish Congress and the Representation of Polish Jewry, *Lest We Forget: The Massacre of the Warsaw Ghetto; A Compilation of Reports* (New York: Spett Printing, 1943).

6. The attempted roundup occurred between 18 January and 22 January 1943. Stroop's predecessor, the SS and Police Leader in the Warsaw District Ferdinand von Sammern-Frankenegg, wanted to "resettle" 16,000 Jewish workers in the Lublin camp complex. However, only 6,000 Jews were captured because of armed resistance by the Jewish Fighting Organization (*Zydowska Organizacja Bojowa*, or ZOB).

7. In a special directive issued on 31 July 1942, Himmler ordered that the word "partisans" be dropped from all reports. The text of Himmler's directive is found in Josef Wulf, *Das Dritte Reich und seine Vollstrecker: Die Liquidation von 500,000 Juden im Ghetto Warschau* (Berlin-Grunewald: Arani Verlag, 1961), p. 68, n.1.

8. The He-halutz movement was a youth movement of Zionist pioneers who had trained to become future kibbutz settlers in Palestine.

9. The text of this poster, which was published in German and Polish, reads as follows:

To the populace of Warsaw! Recently, a large number of murderous attacks have been committed in the city of Warsaw. The same hand, whose work was visible in the mass graves of Polish officers found in Katyn, is also behind these murders. All of these Communist bandits have found refuge in the former Jewish quarter of Warsaw and received extensive help and full support there. The former Jewish quarter has thus been turned into a nest for all supporters of the Bolshevik ideology, who strive to disseminate unrest and subversion among the population. The former Jewish quarter will be destroyed, as will the hopes of the Commune, which delude themselves with the belief that the days of bloody Bolshevik rule will also come to this country. It is the duty of every individual to make provocations by Communist agents and Jews impossible. Every Jew and Bolshevik who today still lives in freedom is an extremely dangerous enemy of the people. No ethical considerations should now be an obstacle to the destruction of Bolshevism, which again reveals its true face with typical terrorist attacks against Warsaw. The civilian population again laments numerous deaths and heavy damages to private property. Whoever informs officials about Communist agents of Jews still at liberty merely fulfills a self-evident duty for himself and his family.
Warsaw, 13 May 1943
                                                                    Dr. Fischer

Dr. Ludwig Fischer was Governor of the Warsaw District at the time. This poster is quoted in full in J. Wulf, *Das Dritte Reich*, p. 91, n.27. (English translation by Sybil Milton)

In his report, Stroop's reference to recent assassinations probably alludes to the execution of a number of Gestapo agents and Jewish informers by the ZOB Command and the Jewish Military Union (the *Zydowski Zwiazek Wojskowy*, or ZEW) during February and March 1943. *See* Reuben Ainsztein, *Jewish Resistance in Nazi-Occupied Eastern Europe* (New York: Barnes & Noble, 1974), p. 576.

10. The recipient of Stroop's daily reports was SS General and General of the Police Friedrich Wilhelm Krueger. He was born in Strassburg in 1894, the son of a colonel. He attended but did not graduate from the Gymnasium in Rastatt. He attended the military academies in Karlsruhe and Gross-Lichterfelde. (The latter was the German equivalent of Sandhurst.) He served in World War I, rising to the rank of first lieutenant. He fought in the Free Corps from 1918 to 1920, and worked as a businessman during the 1920s. He joined the Nazi party in 1929, and the SA and SS in 1931. After 1934, Krueger served exclusively in the SS; however, he was also a member of the *Reichstag* (national parliament) and held Berlin municipal and Prussian state offices. His service in the SS was first in Berlin and after 1935 at the Brown House in Munich. In October 1939 he was appointed Higher SS and Police Leader in Lodz. The next month, Krueger moved to Cracow to occupy the same office for the General Government, simultaneously serving in Hans Frank's cabinet. He left Cracow in November 1943. After serving briefly on Himmler's personal staff, he was transferred to the Balkans in January 1944. In May of that year, he commanded a Waffen-SS

division and in August headed a Waffen-SS corps. He committed suicide in Libau, Latvia, on 9 May 1945.

This biographical sketch is based on Krueger's SS Personnel File in the Berlin Document Center and is reproduced in J. Wulf, *Das Dritte Reich*, pp. 225–38.

11. Max Jesuiter was Stroop's Chief of Staff in Warsaw and countersignator of the daily reports. He was born in Stettin in 1897 and lived in Berlin, where he worked as a salesman. He joined the NSDAP (National Socialist German Workers Party) in 1931 and the SS in 1932. *See* J. Wulf, *Das Dritte Reich*, p. 44.

12. Poniatowo was a subsidiary labor camp of the Lublin Concentration Camp system.

13. Walter Caspar Toebbens was one of the major German employers of over 10,000 Jewish workers in the Warsaw Ghetto; his factories produced military uniforms. With the expropriation and Aryanization of Jewish property, Toebbens became an entrepreneur and acquired at low costs seven Jewish stores in Bremen. In 1939, Toebbens moved into the Warsaw Ghetto. His labor force cost him virtually nothing, and he charged his Jewish workers huge sums of money for certificates protecting them from deportation. After Himmler's January 1943 visit to Warsaw, he wanted to audit the immense profits of Toebbens's works, but nothing ever came of this. In November 1946, Toebbens escaped from a train while being extradited to Poland for war crimes. He was tried in absentia in May 1949 by a Bremen Denazification Tribunal and sentenced to ten years in a labor camp.

Biographical information about Toebbens and his factories can be found in J. Wulf, *Das Dritte Reich*, pp. 87–89, 336–39; and G. Reitlinger, *The Final Solution*, pp. 70, 516.

14. PPR, or the *Polska Partia Robotnicza* (Polish Workers' Party), was the illegal Communist party founded in occupied Poland in January 1942.

15. *Volksdeutsche* were German minorities who lived outside the Reich, such as the Volga Germans or the Sudeten Germans.

16. SB was the designation used by the German authorities for various ranks of policemen serving in the Order Police. *See* Hans-Joachim Neufeldt, Juergen Huck, and Georg Tessin, *Zur Geschichte der Ordnungspolizei, 1936–1945*, v.3, Als Manuskript gedruckt (Koblenz, West Germany: Schriften des Bundesarchivs, 1957), p. xi.

In other contexts, SB also denotes *Schutzmannschafts-Battalion*. *Schutzmannschaft* was the name given to native uniformed police recruited and commanded by the Germans in the eastern occupied territories. *See* Helmut Heiber, ed., *Reichsfuehrer! Briefe an und von Himmler* (Munich: Deutscher Taschenbuch Verlag, 1970), p. 201.

17. Treblinka II was one of the major extermination camps, located on the Bug River about fifty miles from Warsaw.

18. When Stroop refers to the Jewish-Polish defense unit, he probably means the Jewish Fighting Organization.

19. B. Hallmann's furniture factory was one of the centers of Jewish resistance in February 1943. Only 25 of 1,000 Jewish workers reported voluntarily for "resettlement." *Cf.* R. Ainsztein, *Jewish Resistance in Nazi-Occupied Eastern Europe*, p. 617.

20. Fort Traugutta was a park and fortress located outside the Ghetto on the left bank of the Vistula River.

21. Transavia and Wisniewski-Serejski were two factories located, respectively, at 36 Stawki Street and 51 Stawki Street in the Ghetto, where Jews were employed in the repair of aircraft parts.

22. Stroop means the Jewish Fighting Organization.

23. The Prosta has been called the miniature or dwarf ghetto.

24. Stroop is referring to someone who had escaped from Lublin (a city in eastern Poland) or from a transport to Majdanek, officially known as the Lublin Concentration Camp.

25. The "so-called library" refers to the Jewish Institute at 5 Tlomackie Street.

26. Stroop is probably referring to a letter that endorsed his policy. At Katyn in 1943, the Germans discovered mass graves containing the bodies of approximately 4,000 Polish officers who had been shot.

27. Stroop is referring to the ZOB Command bunker located at 18 Mila Street and the death of Mordechai Anielewicz, the Commander of the Jewish Fighting Organization.

28. The ZWZ, or *Zwiazek Walki Zbrojnej* (Armed Struggle Union), was founded as an underground Polish military organization in February 1940 under the command of Colonel Stefan Rowecki. Later, in 1943, it became known as the *Armia Krajowa* (Home Army). Since this organization did not fight in the Ghetto and helped Jews only to a limited extent, it is clear that Stroop once again means the ZOB. It is probable that Stroop's confusion is deliberate, since he had to rationalize the fact that the small, underarmed Jewish forces could oppose the German Army and Police for almost two weeks.

29. OFK is possibly an abbreviation for *Oberfeldkommandantur*, a military body responsible for provisioning and supplies behind each front.

30. The heaviest Soviet Air Force raid on Warsaw occurred during the night on 13–14 May 1943.

31. Maximillian von Herff was Chief of the SS Central Office for Personnel.

He later served as Higher SS and Police Leader on the Russian Central Front. He was executed at Minsk on 6 February 1948. *See* Reitlinger, *The Final Solution*, p. 509.

32. These figures were roughly $5,500 and $6,250–$7,500. Five prewar 1939 zlotys were worth $1.00. In April 1943, about 800 zlotys were equal to that amount. A comparison of prewar and 1943 prices for food is found in Władysław Bartoszewski, *1859 Dsni Warszawy* [*1859 Days in Warsaw*] (Cracow: Wydawnictwo Znak, 1974), p. 374 ff. The Polish text was translated for me by Lucjan Dobroszycki of the YIVO Institute, New York.

33. There is no visual evidence that these men were rabbis, but they were religious Jews in traditional dress and side-locks.

34. *Askaris* were native African soldiers in the service of European powers during World War I. In the Warsaw Ghetto, this name was used for foreign ethnic forces who served with the SS, such as the Ukrainian and Baltic Police units and the Trawniki men.

MAPS

MAP OF THE WARSAW GHETTO
(Opposite Page)

▬ BOUNDARIES, AS ESTABLISHED OCTOBER 15, 1940

With time the Ghetto boundaries were redrawn, making the Ghetto smaller. At the time of the "grand operation," the remaining population was concentrated in three fragments of the former Ghetto, comprising A—the remnant Ghetto *(Restghetto)*, B—a factories area referred to in the *Stroop Report* as "the uninhabited but still restricted Ghetto...containing several armament plants and the like," and C—the Prosta, a section in the former miniature Ghetto (the Ghetto below Choldna Street). It should be noted that the literature sometimes refers to two or all three of these sections as the remnant or remaining Ghetto. Also, not only area B but all three areas contained armament and other war-related German factories that drew on the Jews as laborers.

A

B

C

D MURANOWSKI SQUARE
E WARSAW SYNAGOGUE
F DZIELNA PRISON
G ARMY QUARTERMASTER BUILDINGS on the site of the brush factory
H W.C. TOEBBENS, SCHULTZ & CO., HOFFMANN, and the former
     HALLMANN ENTERPRISE; and TOEBBENS in the miniature Ghetto
I JEWISH CEMETERY
J HEADQUARTERS OF THE ZOB (Zydowska Organizacja Bojowa/Jewish
     Fighting Organization), 18 Mila Street
K FORT and PARK TRAUGUTTA
L ARMAMENT WORKS TRANSAVIA AND WISNIEWSKI (located
     respectively at 36 and 51 Stawki Street)
M THE LIBRARY, Jewish Institute, 5 Tlomackie Street
N BRAUER CO., Nalewski Street and Franciszanska Street
O THE *UMSCHLAGPLATZ* (the cargo area for transshipment of goods at the
     railroad station for Danzig, where the Jews had to assemble for deportation)

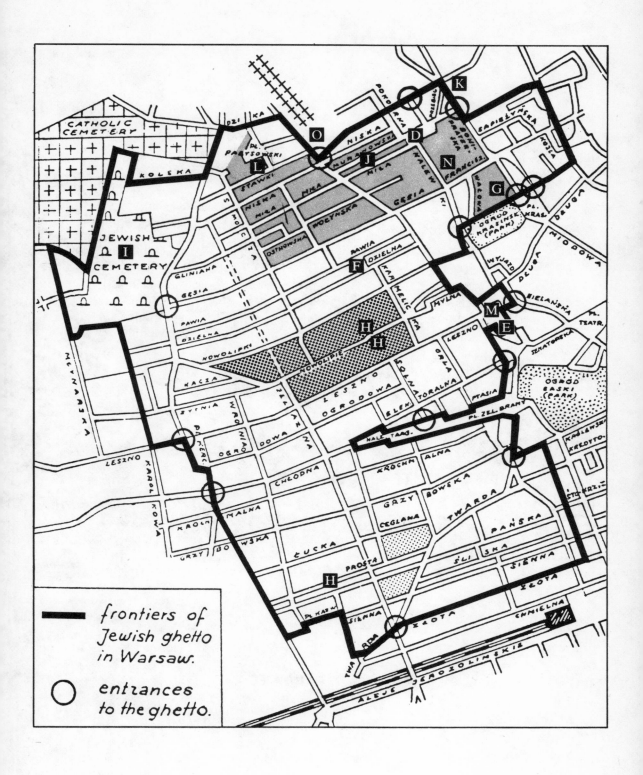

frontiers of Jewish ghetto in Warsaw.

entrances to the ghetto.

WARSAW

——— GHETTO,
AS ESTABLISHED
OCTOBER 15, 1940

The author of this report was SS-Major General Juergen, neé Josef Stroop. He was born in 1895 in the northwest German provincial capital of Detmold, the son of a policeman. During World War I he attained the rank of sergeant. Until he joined the Nazi party and SS in 1932, he was a clerk in the land registry bureau of his native state of Lippe. In 1939 he advanced to SS-Oberfuehrer (Brigadier-General and Colonel of the Police) and was posted to the Sudetenland. After the occupation of Poland in September 1939, Stroop was transferred to Poznan as head of the German Selbstschutz (self-defense units of ethnic Germans). He was promoted to SS-Brigadefuehrer (Major-General) and posted to Berlin in 1940, where he organized special anti-subversion and terrorism units. In March 1943, he was sent as an anti-partisan expert to Galicia. He was then transferred to Warsaw, where he directed the destruction of the Warsaw Ghetto from 19 April through 16 May 1943 and was awarded the Iron Cross First Class for his role. In September 1943, he was detailed to Greece to fight the growing partisan movement, and finally in 1944 Stroop became SS-Chief of Police in Rhein-Westmark.

He was sentenced to death by a U.S. military court in Dachau in 1947 for the shooting of American airmen but extradited to Poland. Tried in Warsaw in 1951, he was again sentenced to death and hanged.

Andrzej Wirth

Literary and drama critic, translator, professor of comparative literature and drama, Andrzej Wirth was born in Poland in 1927· and was cultural editor of the Warsaw weekly *Polityka* and drama critic of the Warsaw weekly *Nowa Kultura*. A collaborator of Brecht's Berliner Ensemble (1956–57), a member of Gruppe 47, he has taught since 1966 at Stanford, the City University of New York, and Harvard. He is at present on the faculty of the Free University of Berlin and a senior associate member of St. Antony's College, Oxford.